C000063174

ACKNOWLEDGEMENTS

To that bottle of Fitou, thank you. My life changed for the better the moment I drained the last drop.

To that Turkish bar, thank you for being there. That night changed all our lives for good.

To the best wife I could ever have had, thank you more than words can ever say. For everything you do for me. And for raising two amazing kids.

To Rory and Roonagh, thank you for being the lights of my life. The trip wouldn't have happened without you.

To Michael Heppell, international best-selling author, I couldn't have done this without your support, guidance and encouragement. You are brilliant.

To Ana Elisa Alcocer Zubiría, thank you for the beautiful and creative illustrations in this book. I hope readers love them as much as I do.

To Kim MacLeod of Indie Authors World, thank you for your talent and energy in helping me get this book released into the wild.

To everyone who inspired me to write this book, who challenged, encouraged and supported me, thank you.

Now it's written, what's the worst that can happen?

Are We There Yet?

Ian Pilbeam

Great People
Publishing

Published in 2021 by Great People Publishing

Copyright © 2021 Ian Pilbeam

Ian Pilbeam has asserted his right to be identified as the author of this Work in accordance with the Copyright, Designs and Patents Act 1988

ISBN Paperback: 978-1-8383882-0-1
Ebook: 978-1-8383882-1-8

A CIP catalogue copy of this book can be found in the British Library.

Published with the help of Indie Authors World
www.indieauthorsworld.com

The year-long adventure that kept on giving

ARE YOU MAD?

One night in a Turkish bar

"Where would you like to go next kids?" Little did I know, but this simple question was about to change our lives forever.

The scene: an ordinary tourist bar in southern Turkey. Classic Brits abroad fare.

An unassuming family of 2.4 kids, minus the point four, hailing from Bonnie Scotland. Three Scots and an English dad who knows his neeps from his tatties.

Meet Ian, later known as *Papa Tripper*, Anne, who would become *Mama Tripper*, and the two stars of the story, Rory age nine and Roonagh age seven. Just an ordinary family who would go on to do extraordinary things thanks to this seductive question.

"Where would you like to go next kids?"

The answer took me by surprise. These kids were mature beyond their years.

"Can we have a think about that Daddy and come back tomorrow with some ideas?"

Their response was unexpected. My glass was ready to be refilled, so I took this innocent response at face value and went to the bar.

Fast forward 24 hours. Same bar, same family. As the waiter cleared away our plates, the kids smiled sheepishly and brandished a folded-up sheet of paper.

"Daddy, we've been thinking, and these are the places we would like to go to next please." They may have said "*please*." Let's assume they did. I would like to think we brought them up properly.

Intrigued, I opened the sheet of paper to find a list of countries they would like to visit. But not any old list, because next to the name of each country was an animal. It went something like this

Madagascar- Lemurs

Australia- Kangaroos

Canada- Polar bears

Africa- Cheetahs

China- Pandas

Peru- Llamas

Galápagos Islands- Iguanas

Cyprus

Why animals? No one knows. They can't remember and I never asked. I guess they were children, and most kids love fluffy and furry animals. I had resisted requests throughout their childhoods to buy them a puppy. Perhaps this was their way of wreaking their revenge on me?

I do know why Cyprus was on the list. It was nothing to do with animals. Quite simply, our daughter's first teacher, Mrs Kalamidis, had retired there. Roonagh loved Mrs Kalamidis.

We looked at the list agog. "Wow what a list. We would love to go to those places as well. They sound amazing."

I turned to Anne and remarked, "I wonder if you can get round the world tickets for families?"

I would like to think we were already a global family. Anne had spent a year in France with her language teacher parents when she was ten. My first overseas flight was at the age of 17, an exchange programme in Spain. By the time the trip was over, the kids would each have visited 50 countries. How the world has shrunk.

I studied languages at University and believed my destiny would be a career as a professional linguist. However, during a French lecture in my final term, a lecturer said "Ian, you speak French like Inspector Clouseau speaks English." Instantly, I knew my future career as an interpreter at the United Nations was doomed.

Travel had sealed my future life with Anne 15 years previously. One year into our relationship, we booked a two week package holiday to Tunisia. We quickly became stir crazy, cooped up inside an all-inclusive complex. Many side trips and adventures were soon booked in the Atlas Mountains. We were kindred spirits. We both had restless souls, a curiosity for the world, and an urge to travel that would shape our lives.

Shortly after our return home, I fell on one knee and proposed. A potent bottle of Fitou, a strong French red wine, may have been involved, but we both knew we had found *the one*. The rest, as they say, is history

Within a few years, we had two young children. Initially, we resorted to traditional holidays, trips in the car down to France, reminiscent of the summer breaks of Anne's childhood. In time, we branched out to a couple of more adventurous holidays in Sri Lanka and Morocco. We also enjoyed, or should I say endured, an all-inclusive holiday in St Lucia in the Caribbean. Much like the Tunisian experience, we were eager to escape through the security gates and explore the real island. The travel bug was a real and present danger from the start of our relationship

The seeds were sown, ingredients bought, and recipe written for a family who would not stop travelling. Maybe that night in that Turkish bar was fate giving us the boot up the backside we needed.

There was another tragic catalyst for the decision, relating to Anne's parents. The same folk who had taken her to France for a year when she was just ten. And who had supported her decision, as a 15 year old girl, to spend a summer as an Au Pair in the Pyrenees. And had to cope with me as a son-in-law, even if the Father of the Bride speech at our Wedding Breakfast did contain the heartfelt line, "*I never thought my daughter would marry an Englishman.*"

Sue and Jack still had many years ahead of them. At least that's what should have happened. They met at Teacher Training College when Sue was just 20, and Jack was 40 years old. Perhaps because of the age gap, they had saved responsibly, underpinned by generous public sector pensions. Sue would enjoy a long retirement, even after Jack's passing in the way distant future. However, this was not to be.

We moved into the same village as my in-laws with two young children, just five minutes' walk from their bungalow directly opposite the local school.

"That's childcare sorted for the next 20 years" I glibly told Anne. To illustrate the point, we left both children in Sue and Jack's capable hands and took a romantic trip to Paris.

Anne called Sue to check the kids were ok. "I have some slightly worrying news" said Sue. "I have had a rectal bleed and am in hospital. But don't worry."

At that moment, time stood still. Everything stopped. Sue was diagnosed with terminal bowel cancer at just 55 years-old.

Shortly afterwards, Jack, now in his mid-70s, had a series of strokes, resulting in vascular dementia. We agreed to sell their home and ours and move in together so we could look after Jack for as long as possible.

Caring for Jack significantly impacted on family life. Confused, he would ask the kids "why are you going upstairs in someone else's house" and sometimes wander down the street to "*go home*." Family outings became impossible, apart from occasional breaks thanks to respite care.

The upside of this tragedy was that we were financially secure and mortgage-free. This security played a crucial role in our conversations in that Turkish resort.

I looked at Anne and asked, "Should we do it? Should we take the kids around the world?"

I expected her to put me in my place with retorts such as "get a grip" or "don't be ridiculous." But she replied, "Why not, what's the worst that can happen, we have to sell the house and downsize."

Those were the words I needed to hear. The impulsive part of my personality was in overdrive.

In my head I thought *I want to go to Madagascar. I want to go to Australia, home of Kylie Minogue. I want to go to Peru.* Since childhood, I had dreamed of going to Deepest Darkest Peru, home of Paddington Bear and his Great Aunt Lucy.

Suddenly all bets were off and it was a remote possibility. The next morning, we were back in the same bar. We pulled out some lira, paid the barman for the privilege of using the desktop computer, cranked up the dial-up connection and searched. And there it was. It was feasible. There were companies offering round the world tickets for families. Not only that, but we wouldn't be the first. We found blogs of other families who had done it already. "Wow. This might just be possible" we said. Over the remainder of the holiday, we talked the idea through many times. Crazy or Genius? Fantasy or Reality?

I have always believed that life is a book. It is up to each author now many chapters the book has, and how interesting they are. I was beginning to see that a year around the world with the kids would provide us with amazing chapters of our own books.

As Jack's health deteriorated, our home ceased to provide a safe environment for him. The impact on the kids and our family life was also too severe. Fortunately, a room became available in a nearby care home just before our Turkish holiday.

When we got home, we visited him, and as we left the care home, I uttered these harsh but true words, "If we do this, he won't actually know whether we're here or not." Sad but true.

Anne replied "And we have just had such an amazing two weeks with the kids, what would a year be like? This could be just the thing our family needs."

Sue had saved for a retirement she never reached. We could put the money we had inherited aside, and enjoy it in a retirement we may or may not reach, or we could invest it now. Invest in our family, in our children and ourselves.

I said to Anne, "this investment will have a long-term impact on all of us, collectively and individually. I don't know what that means yet and we will find out maybe in ten years' time, but we will find out." They were prophetic words.

Within three weeks of our return, I was negotiating my exit from a job I loved, my first ever role as an HR Director. Within three months my leaving party had been enjoyed, my P45 issued and I was unemployed, cast astray by my own fair hand.

"Hey Kids, remember that list of countries you came up with on holiday this summer? Well we are going to go on a big trip and see them all."

We were walking to school one crisp late Autumn morning, hand in hand. The kids were still at an age where it was cool to hold Daddy's hand. Roonagh replied, "Will we be able to go to them all in two weeks Daddy?" Bless, the innocence of a child. I explained they would miss a whole year of school to go around the world. I am not sure they really understood, but what kid would turn down the opportunity to skip class for an entire year?

Roonagh believed she would sleep every night in a Premier Inn, a purple roomed British hotel chain. During her final term at school, she studied earthquakes and had nightmares about us all dying in Japan. Much reassurance was needed. We certainly didn't tell her about the massive earthquake in China just a few weeks before we left, a natural disaster that would have a significant impact on our trip, in ways we could not foresee.

This little family had a plan. It was a plan that would hold us in good stead, although as with all good plans, it was subject to frequent change.

No plan survives first contact with the enemy. So said the often-quoted 19th-century Prussian military commander Helmuth van Moltke. He may not have had family travel at the forefront of his mind, but if the cap fits Helmuth, wear it.

Why oh why?

We were asked many questions at the time and many more since.

Most often thought, but never asked in our presence, was "Are you mad?" Many of our friends just didn't get it.

Here are some other questions we were asked:

"How did you choose where to go?"

"Where was your favourite place?"

"Where was your least favourite place?"

"What about the kids' education?"

"How did you travel?"

"What impact did it have on your lives?"

My least favourite has to be "Did you enjoy your holiday?" Believe me, travelling for a year with your kids is many things, but it most certainly is not a holiday.

The question that needed answering first was "Where would we go to in our year away?"

How on earth do you choose which places to go for an entire year? Before long, as I immersed myself in travel guides and the internet, I was wondering, Why is it only a year, could it not be longer? Several factors influenced where we ended up going.

The first was the kid's list. The list they produced in that bar in Turkey.

We didn't go to all of those destinations, but it was clear that wherever we would go needed to be somewhere the kids would enjoy, be child friendly and safe. That helped to narrow things down.

Our first destination was always going to be Cape Town. In my student days, the anti-apartheid struggle in South Africa was in full throttle, and as a young man, this became my cause juste. In 1988, I attended Nelson Mandela's 70th birthday party at Wembley Stadium. Mandela had been in prison for 26 years, and the world did not even know what he looked like. Two years later, I was back at Wembley, and this time a free Mandela was on stage to address the ecstatic masses.

Fifteen years later I participated in a hike in South Africa, raising money for a Scottish cancer charity in tribute to my mother-in-law Sue, followed by a further highly enjoyable week in Cape Town with some other trekkers. The highlight was an emotional visit to Robben Island, where Mandela had been imprisoned. The only place we could start our year around the world was the foot of Africa.

I have always liked bookends and loved the idea of starting in an iconic city by the sea with a famous mountain. And finishing in one. It soon emerged that 52 weeks after arriving in Cape Town, we would head for home from Rio de Janeiro. From Cape Town to Rio, that had a nice ring to it.

We wanted to visit as many continents as we could. Why not? Europe was on our doorstep and we could go there anytime. On cost grounds, we excluded North America. That left Africa, Asia, Oceania and South America. We fancied all of these.

The round the world ticket required us to travel in either a clockwise or anti-clockwise direction. We surmised that clockwise presented fewer jet lag challenges. The rules restricted us to a maximum of five flights per continent. From this framework, a plan started to emerge. Decisions came down to a combination of desire and logistics, including the weather.

The world's climate is volatile. Monsoons, hurricanes and extreme heat should be avoided, especially when travelling with kids. The only one of these meteorological events I didn't completely avoid in my planning was the heat. We come from Scotland so fancied a bit of sun, but not too much. Some family members need to protect their pale blue skin with Factor 50 SPF when it is 15 degrees centigrade outside.

I spent many hours of my life, sometimes entire days, researching places we might visit. Thank goodness I was now unemployed. Planning filled the days. Most of these far-off destinations never made the cut. I learnt a great deal though and could easily curate another year away. Who knows, maybe one day I will.

I loved that we could visit places that were an impossibility when I was younger. South Africa, the scene of the horrors of apartheid during my formative years. Cambodia, which I had seen through the grisly prism of the book and movie *The Killing Fields*. Vietnam, the setting for Oliver Stone movies and Springsteen songs, and Chile, former domain of the Dictator General Pinochet and land of *Los Desaparecidos* which I had studied at University.

Many travel blogs were devoured. A ridiculous number of questions posted on travel forums. Research, Research, Research.

Starting in Southern Africa meant we would end our year in South America.

We had a list of destinations and we had a route. Next, we needed to put timings on it. How long would we stay in each place?

The only open-jaw leg was into Kuala Lumpur, leaving three months later from Singapore. There were plenty of overland options and cheap local airlines. We fancied the flexibility and opportunities for spontaneity this would provide.

There was a surprise at the planning stage when we booked our flight itinerary. The travel agent pointed out we had one extra flight available to us in Africa. He explained the options, one of which was Mauritius.

I had always thought of Mauritius as a honeymoon destination, so it didn't instantly appeal. A year on the road with the kids would not be particularly romance friendly. But then I saw that Mauritius was next to Madagascar. One of the places on the kids' list due to the lemurs. As it would do many times more, the plan changed. I yelled downstairs, "Kids, we are going to Madagascar!"

We needed an identity as a travelling family, a name to cement us together. Us against the world. Simply being called *The Pilbeams* would not be enough. I invented the name *Family Trippers*. I still have no idea where it came from, but I like things that do what they say on the tin.

If we were to be the *Family Trippers*, then I would be *Papa Tripper* and Anne would be *Mama Tripper*. And then, of course, we had *Rory Tripper* and *Roonagh Tripper*. Suddenly we had our names and an identity.

I was inspired by the travel blogs I read online. They seemed to be a great way of capturing the journey for posterity. A website would get our name out and perhaps inspire other like-minded families to follow in our footsteps. The Family Trippers website was conceived and would host all the blogs I wrote over the course of the year and some special ones from the kids. Without these blogs, some of the connections and experiences which later came our way would not have happened.

Blogs were written with one eye knowing that those back home, who worried about us, would read them. Mum and Dad, you know who you are. They were therefore ever so slightly sanitised and didn't capture all the lows and scary moments we experienced. For example, in the blog about our wonderful time in the Galápagos Islands, you won't find the story of how one of our children nearly drowned. Or the episode when we believed we had been kidnapped by Chinese mafia. But these stories will feature in this book. We want to tell the story, the whole story and nothing but the story.

Who are we? In all honesty, we are a quiet and unassuming family. We are not loud or brash, and we don't have a huge circle of friends. But we are curious. I hope in the right meaning of the word. The world fascinates us. We are intrigued by its people, and by the infinite diversity of the planet we are blessed to have the opportunity to inhabit.

At the time of our travels, we were all vegetarian. This would have a significant impact on our experiences on the road. Many inexpensive meals in McDonalds, a mainstay for other backpackers, were not an option for us, although we did make good use of their toilet facilities. We shall explore the long-term impact the experience of a year's family travel had on the kids, but it is perhaps no coincidence that they are now vegan. The trip taught them to be kind and to care in an essentially different way than if they had only learnt these values at home and school. This is reflected in the values they have taken into adulthood.

As for me, your trusty guide on this intrepid journey, I have pursued a modest career in Human Resources and now run my own outsourcing business. I am passionate about travel, obviously. The trip dramatically impacted on me, particularly my tolerance for risk.

What's the worst that can happen? We have to sell the house and downsize.

Without the trip, I would not have had the courage to start my own business.

What's the worst that can happen? My new business fails, and I have to get another job.

No trip, no business. No business, no book. Without the experience and connections gained in running a business, I would never have got around to setting out our life-changing experiences in this way.

"*She may be small but she is fierce*" wrote William Shakespeare in *A Midsummer Night's Dream*. What an apt description for my wee bonnie lassie, Anne or *Annie*. I tend to say I took my kids around the world for a year. The truth is Anne took the kids around the world, me and the younger two. I am one lucky guy.

We don't need no education

Thank goodness we didn't travel with teenagers. I have nothing against teenagers. I was once one myself.

We met a few families with adolescents on the road. They generally appeared miserable, exhausted and hormonal. Their parents looked frustrated, distracted and wishing they were elsewhere. One travelling parent told us how their hormonal teenage son had ruined their day at Machu Picchu by just not being in the mood, generously deflecting their teenage angst onto the rest of the family on what should have been for them, as it was for us, the best of days.

Some families travel with pre-school children. In many ways, this is even braver.

Imagine travelling with all the paraphernalia which accompanies a young child.

Imagine travelling in a permanent state of sleep deprivation.

Imagine travelling while coping with childhood illnesses in far-flung places.

And then there's the *terrible twos*.

How impactful and memorable would the investment in this experience be if the kids couldn't even remember it. Huge kudos to those parents, but it would never have been for us.

It was luck, or perhaps fate that our kids were the age they were when we took the trip. We hadn't planned it this way, it was just how things panned out. They were eight and ten when we left, and nine and eleven when we got back. To this day, I believe this was the ideal age from a parental perspective. They were not yet hormonal, they still respected and maybe on occasions even idolised us. We would joke about *Daddy's special paw*, my left hand, which always had a child attached to it no matter where we were. I was still *Daddy*, and Anne was still *Mummy*. Hugs and kisses were welcomed, not embarrassing.

From an educational point of view, this was the perfect age for them to skip school. They were not yet into a full curriculum. There were no exams nor qualifications to worry about.

The most common questions we were asked were, "Did you home school them?" or "How did you educate them?"

The simple answer is that the world was their classroom. They could read, they could write, and had a basic grasp of numeracy. They observed and assimilated learning from their surroundings. Finding suitable books on the road was a challenge in a pre-Kindle age so we would obsessively scour second-hand bookshops and charity stores for age-appropriate content. The kids ended up reading horizon-broadening books they would never have discovered otherwise.

With Maths, it was merely a case of keeping on top of the basics. Walks in the jungle or on a beach would provide an opportunity to recite times tables. Rory would on occasions take responsibility for the daily budget, even if it were just adding up in his head how much we'd spent. There were times when I would come to regret this decision. As our financial controller, he would take great pleasure in telling me when the daily budget was overspent and I was not permitted to indulge in the beer I craved.

He also became our walking currency converter. At school, they call this *Mental Maths*. He did the maths, and I uploaded the results into a spreadsheet on my laptop.

As part of on the road schooling, we decided the kids should each write a daily diary. They rarely thanked us for this opportunity. In the early days, their scribblings often consisted of little more than *We watched The Simpsons, had pasta for tea and went to bed*. Their nagging parents didn't let them get away with this for long. As the trip went by, the diaries became more descriptive and on occasions were truly stunning.

The curriculum for the year was amazing. The kids learnt so much they would never have been taught at school.

Ready, Steady, Go

We didn't go on the trip immediately. It was important for the kids to finish the academic year, which would take us up until the end of June. Ironically, taking them out of school for a week is technically illegal, yet a full year was permissible. Fortunately, the school was very supportive. Their teachers were ever so slightly jealous.

I was conscious I had not travelled independently before. No gap year nor inter-railing around Europe, unlike many of my student peers. I was naïve when it came to travel and Anne was in the same boat. I knew I needed to learn travel skills. After all, I was going to have my children's lives in my hands.

An opportunity presented itself for me to spend three months volunteering for a charity in Sri Lanka before we left. I was part of a community of British volunteers, some of whom were experienced travellers. I soaked up everything as they shared their experiences, tricks and tips. The family came out to join me at the end of the three months. We had a trip around the island and a dry run at being a travelling family.

On our return home, we packed down our house, which we had successfully rented out to a Church Minister and got ready to go. The family cat, an overweight and temperamental creature called Hattie, was to stay at a kind neighbour's house. I released her into their garden, she bolted, jumped over the hedge and was never seen again. It took a while before I plucked up the courage to break the news to the animal obsessed Roonagh.

We had to move out two weeks before the trip because the Minister and his family needed to be in early. Not ideal but hardly a massive problem either. We were so pleased to have the house occupied, and the rental income would come in handy. We spent many long evenings putting our belongings into boxes. Our furniture went to a removal company, with remaining items dispersed between our loft and neighbours' garages. Our brand-new rucksacks were weighed and weighed again. We carried a lighter load around the world than we had on that Turkish holiday the previous summer.

There was no going back. A caravan in a nearby holiday camp became home for two weeks. We started the trip on our doorstep.

I remember well the morning we left the caravan park to travel down to my parents, where we would leave my car before getting the train to London and on to Heathrow for our first flight.

As we woke on that summer's morning, we discovered Roonagh had vomited spectacularly all over her bedding and room. When I say vomit, I mean monumentally upchucked. All up the wall. Which was of course covered with wallpaper, flocked wallpaper, which held the chunks of spew really well. And there were copious amounts. She always did this when she was excited. And we were all excited. Past tense. At this moment, excitement was not our predominant emotion. She also threw up all over her favourite cuddly toy *Spotty* who never quite regained her youthful fluffiness.

What a start. Detergent out and marigold gloves on, furious mopping and wiping ensued. We were supposed to be on the road by now. Bundling up the bedding, we handed it over to an unsuspecting cleaner and proffered a million apologies.

We squeezed Roonagh and her repulsed brother into an overpacked car, comprising us, our rucksacks and various valuables to be deposited for safekeeping at my parents' house. We placed a washing up bowl on her lap, wound down the windows to let the delightful smell of vomit dissipate into the early morning Scottish air, and off we set. Leaving Scotland, knowing we would not be back for another 12 months.

"Let's go kids."

Our final weekend in the UK was spent at my parents' house, where I would leave the car for a year in a local farmer's barn, the same farm where I had worked every summer during my teenage years. Another bookend moment.

It just so happened that weekend was Nelson Mandela's 90th birthday party concert in Hyde Park. I had also seen Mandela speak at the launch of the *Make Poverty History* campaign in 2005. This would be the third and final time I would see him in the flesh.

I will never forget leaving my parents' house 48 hours after the concert. She may have been tearful, but my mother held herself together admirably. My father looked worried. The final words he said to me before we departed were, "Please look after my grandchildren, won't you." If I didn't appreciate the weight of responsibility on my shoulders already, I did now.

Ironically, the kids had never been to London. We left our bags for a few hours at the left luggage facility at Kings Cross Station, grabbed a family travel-card and did a whistle-stop tour of the city, including a pilgrimage to Mandela's statue in

Parliament Square. We then got the Tube to Heathrow ready for our first flight. The first of 40 flights over the next year.

The Round the World ticket was a booklet of ticket stubs for each flight. There was also an overall voucher. Our travel agent had assured me we did not need to take this. However, being slightly overcautious, I packed it anyway. What a good job. When we arrived at the Departure Gate, we needed it. Had I left it back in Scotland our round the world trip would have consisted of a weekend trip from Edinburgh to London and back again. But all was well. We boarded the overnight flight to Cape Town exhausted, full of anticipation and with no real idea what we were letting ourselves in for.

South Africa
The Adventure Begins

Isn't it amazing when a plan comes together? As we stepped down from the plane, a scarlet sunrise streaked across the horizon. It was a beautiful morning on the first day of our adventure. Sleep had been a stranger during the overnight long-haul flight, but it mattered not as a surging wave of adrenaline coursed through my veins. We stepped onto South African soil for the first time as a family. Only the tentative grip of a child in each hand deterred me from falling to my knees and kissing the tarmac, like a visiting Pontiff at the start of a Papal overseas tour.

Being a true Brit, I checked the weather forecast many times in advance and knew we would need to crack on if we were to ascend Table Mountain. A taxi took us directly to our pre-booked accommodation, we dropped off our bags and walked straight to the cable car station at the foot of this famous mountain. We enjoyed a glorious morning at the top, revelling in iconic views over the city and ocean and feeling like the luckiest family in the world. As we descended, as per the meteorological predictions and bang on time, a thick blanket of cloud known as *the tablecloth* fell. We never saw Table Mountain again during our eight day launchpad break in Cape Town.

When I compiled the initial itinerary, I knew it would be important not to hit the ground too hard too quickly, a bit like breaking in a new pair of shoes. Therefore, our first base was a lovely three-bedroom apartment, making Cape Town feel more like a city break than full-on backpacking. Much like a new pair of hiking boots, we needed breaking in if we were to enjoy, not endure, the year on the road ahead of us.

City break we did, visiting all the tourist attractions the inclement winter weather allowed. It may have been July, but we were in the Southern Hemisphere now, and winter was in full flow. The wet and windy weather meant we spent long hours in museums, a rookie mistake which put the kids off them in week one. On many subsequent occasions, we would need to rely upon museums to kill time, avoid the heat and educate the kids.

Sadly, the weather affected our ability to experience some key visitor destinations during our Cape Town stay.

In the bay, Robben Island, ever-present but temporarily out of sight, was where Mandela was incarcerated for 18 of his 27 years in prison. The stormy weather meant the ferry was cancelled. I was saddened I could not share with my family this essential piece of South African modern history.

We went to see African Penguins hopping around Boulders Beach. The rain lashed down so hard we could not even get out of the car without being immediately soaked. The penguins may have been on the beach, who knows, but through the rain and our car's over-worked windscreen wipers, it was impossible to tell.

The next stop on our planned itinerary for the day was a drive to the Cape of Good Hope. We decided there was little point in making the trip in such awful weather. We adjourned for lunch at a Tibetan restaurant in the nearby naval base of Simonstown where we watched a local troop of baboons wreak havoc as they marauded from house to house and car to car, destroying anything they deemed to be edible or just in their way.

It was also important the kids realised how lucky they were. Before we left home, I had contacted a children's football team in nearby Muizenberg. Due to our friends' generosity, we were carrying an extra bag containing over 50 branded football shirts. Everything from Real Madrid to Falkirk FC. The shirts would be used as prizes for man of the match, most skilful player and fair play awards. They were gratefully received by the team's coach and a couple of players. It was a privilege to do something to help these kids growing up in such difficult circumstances. Unfortunately, the winter weather prevented us from having a kickabout.

I am sure this experience had a lasting impact on the kids. I know it did because a decade later Rory undertook a one month voluntary placement during his University Summer Holiday in the very same place.

I remember saying to Anne in that Turkish bar, "Imagine if, at the end of a holiday, rather than having to get a flight back home, you could jump on a plane to somewhere else, a place you had never been and just keep going."

This felt like an escapist dream which could only happen to others, not to an ordinary family like us. Eight days into our round the world trip, we did this for the first time when we caught an internal flight from Cape Town to Durban.

We left Cape Town in teeming rain and flew 800 miles east and north up to Durban on the Indian Ocean coast. The airline, *Kulula.com*, won our award for *Most Entertaining Cabin Announcement*.

"In the event of a loss of cabin pressure, a free oxygen mask will appear. When you have finished screaming, please place the mask over your face."

"If we have to land on the sea, would those of you who can swim please leave by the exit on the left. To those passengers who cannot swim, thank you for flying with us."

"Please make sure you take all your belongings with you. If you do leave any belongings, please make sure they are ones that the cabin crew will enjoy. No children thank you."

The week gently built up to a crescendo of animal activity. We spent our first three nights in a pleasant chalet at the Dolphin Holiday Resort. Wildlife viewing was limited to the Vervet Monkeys who visited our veranda each morning. What we didn't see were dolphins, neither in the sea nor on the veranda.

Next, we headed up the *Elephant Coast* for the longest walk of Roonagh's life. We were searching for animals in the wild. Not elephants though, we were stalking a herd of eight giraffes. Did you know the collective noun for giraffes is a tower? So actually, we went in search of a tower of giraffe. After three patient(ish) hours, we found such a tower. They were very friendly, and we spent ages watching them. At bedtime, Roonagh declared this day, "The best day of her life."

A couple of days later, I reflected on how it was going so far over a cold beer whilst watching a crimson sunset from the balcony of our tree house at Isinkwe Lodge, deep in the heart of rural South Africa. Yes, I was having a cold beer. Our financial controller, ten-year-old Rory, allowed me this indulgence once in a while.

Isinkwe is Zulu for bushbaby in case you are wondering. The kids were desperate to see unusual animals, including those so endangered it might be now or never. We would see many more exotic creatures during our trip, but the week we had just enjoyed was a decent start. And now included a bushbaby.

That evening we enjoyed a night walk through the nearby woods. Unfortunately, or perhaps luckily, we did not spot any animals. Our guide only told us that we had been looking for scorpions, snakes and spiders after the walk. We stood in awe looking up at the Southern Sky's bright and plentiful stars which, in the absence of light pollution, were a sight to behold.

Our next destination was St Lucia. Not the island in the Caribbean where we had taken an all-inclusive holiday a couple of years previously. Lake St Lucia is Africa's most extensive estuarine system. Home to over 800 hippos and 1,200 crocodiles, it hosts a wide variety of birdlife including a giant heron we saw which was taller than Rory.

A two hour sunset cruise promised sightings of all the above and we were not disappointed. At least 80 hippos and 25 crocodiles were busy going about their daily business. We witnessed a vicious fight between a couple of hippos, engaged in combat like prize fighters at the MGM Grand in Las Vegas. No wonder they kill more men in Africa than any other animal, apart from man himself of course.

Another wow moment was a visit to see cheetahs at an educational project. The fastest of all the big cats, cheetahs were Roonagh's favourite animal, mainly because her best-loved cuddly toy, and our honorary family tripper for the year, was

Spotty. We learnt that female cheetahs have sight recognition which is stronger than their sense of smell.

A female cheetah, fortunately behind a fence, thought that Spotty was an inquisitive cub and went for her. My heart nearly exploded out of my chest. I was holding her at the time and got quite a fright. We moved away quickly, and Spotty spent the rest of the morning well hidden under my jacket.

Roonagh declared that the Tower of Giraffes "was dumped" and this had been the best day of her life.

Then there was our first, but not last safari. The Hluhluwe-Umfolozi Reserve is renowned as one of the best if lesser-known South African game reserves. We were at the main gate for 6:00 am and returned to Isinkwe Lodge 12 hours later, exhausted but exhilarated.

Amongst the classic African animals we saw that fabulous day were rhino, elephant, zebra, giraffe, buffalo and wildebeest. We were also incredibly lucky to spend 20 minutes watching a cheetah prowling by the roadside. This time Spotty stayed safely out of view on the back seat of our car.

We had been fortunate enough to see four of the Big Five in a single day, namely lion, rhino, elephant and buffalo, so we already only had leopard still on our wish list. The Big Five are very different animals from the *Wee Five* back home in Scotland: Golden eagle, red deer, red squirrel, otter and harbour seal. If we spotted them in South Africa, then something would have gone badly awry.

Guess what? Yes, Roonagh decided the cheetah day was also "dumped," and this was the best day of her life.

Our final wildlife experience of this leg was not a cheap one: whale watching. Our most expensive activity to date would blow two days' budget, but we wanted to go whale watching at some point on the trip, and this seemed like the ideal opportunity.

There were several places in St Lucia offering excursions. We shopped around and found one we could afford. What a costly mistake.

Whilst we were in the shop purchasing our tickets, Rory desperately needed to pee. There was a toilet in the corner. Reluctantly the shopkeeper agreed that he could use it on condition that he only did a number one. Rory locked the door behind him and disappeared for what felt like an eternity. The anxious shopkeeper became very agitated.

"He's doing a number 2, he's doing a number two, I said he could only do a number one, no number twos."

To this day Rory swears it was just a *number one*, but I doubt our unfriendly shopkeeper would agree.

The next day we arrived early at the long thin beach on a cold, wet and wild morning. The wind was strong enough to test even the strongest of toupees. We were to board the second sailing of the day. We watched the first boat bounce over the waves, then veer left before heading across the surf parallel to the shoreline. Finally, at 15 metres out, it turned sharply towards the beach and crashed into the sand. It looked terrifying. Rory, just visible under his green hoodie, took off his life jacket, threw it to the ground and exclaimed, "I resign," his face red with anger and blue with cold. But with the money we had paid, there was no way he was dodging this bullet.

On we got, the tiny vessel headed off into the Indian Ocean, and the Family Trippers hung on for dear life. It was not a pleasant experience. The waves were huge, the boat was wee and grown men were throwing up over the side. Not including me, of course.

Our sour shopkeeper had guaranteed we would get our money back if we didn't see any whales. The small print must have been minuscule. According to the boat's spotter, some spouting was visible in the distance at one point. That was enough to ensure we would not receive any refund.

On the way back, I decided to stand with my back to the bow, so I had something to hold and keep me upright. Every time we hit a wave, my back smashed into the railing. Like a fading boxing champion taking one punch too many to the ribs, I must have bruised a kidney because that night, back in the tree lodge, I had to go to the outside toilet 17 times. Yes, 17 times.

"Sorry dear, I need to pop out again." Even for me, 17 trips to the loo in one night is a record, and I'm not known for having a particularly strong bladder.

Swaziland
Mind the gap

Next, it was on to Swaziland, via our first land border crossing which was no more than a couple of huts with a tiny patch of concrete between them. Rather anticlimactic but it did the job.

Swaziland is a small kingdom state with a population of just over one million. It is landlocked within South Africa, as is mountainous Lesotho. Due to the twists and turns of colonial history, Swaziland has never been part of South Africa and was granted independence from the UK in 1968. There were few obvious signs of this colonial past, Swaziland felt very African to us.

The country has one of the world's few remaining absolute monarchies. Tragically, it also has the world's highest incidence of HIV/AIDS. Over a quarter of all those aged between 15 and 49 are HIV positive. Unsurprisingly, despite the wealth of the monarchy, there are crippling levels of poverty.

Heart-breaking evidence was apparent in every village and town we drove through. Piles of empty coffins stacked high, waiting for their next victim. Young children at the side of the road, desperate, gaunt and emaciated with tiny hands outstretched. The pleading faces of two orphans as we pulled out of one beauty spot will haunt me for the rest of my days.

We had nothing to help these unfortunate souls other than hard cash. On previous holidays in the developing world, we had packed simple educational gifts such as pencils and notebooks, but this time there was not enough room in our backpacks. This is a pathetic excuse and not one I am proud of. Our hearts ached and tears flowed.

We spent just three nights in Swaziland at a nature reserve which looked like an African farm park. The accommodation was predominantly traditional beehive huts, but we had splashed out and booked *The Cottage*. For obvious reasons, nothing was expensive in Swaziland, and our limited funds went further than previously.

The cottage was huge, with a cape reed thatch roof, large patio and a separate braai area overlooking the game reserve. Ranging freely around the place were warthog, impala and nyala. Next to the bar was a pool where hippos and crocs lounged. There was a sign next to the bar warning *CROCODILES CAN JUMP OVER 2 METRES! Please Stay Away From The Railings*. Now there's a great way to incentivise social distancing.

We did have one bowel loosening encounter with a hippo whilst in a bird hide with one gigantic specimen snorting directly under our feet. We could see and smell him through the gap in the planks of wood. I would say he was no more than two inches away from our feet. Fortunately, he could not see us. Hippos weigh three tons and can run at breakneck speeds of up to 30 kilometres per hour. I used to do cross country running in my youth, but I would not have stood a chance in a sprint with this fellow.

We made full use of the reserve, including a couple of stunning walks whilst singing the theme tune to *Winnie the Pooh*. We made full use of the braai area where the campsite *fireman* made us a log fire each evening. The first night we attempted a barbecue but were rudely interrupted by a cheeky impala who tucked in, helping himself to veggie burgers, cucumber and beer. My beer, of course, a chilled bottle of Castle Lager I was savouring. What a nerve.

South Africa
Where's the leopard?

Kruger National Park was next up on our packed itinerary, via a functional side trip to a small border town just eight kilometres from both Kruger and Mozambique. We were eight kilometres from Mozambique and didn't go. I still regret that. I also regret using the hostel laundry and later discovering several items of our clothing had mysteriously gone missing. Lesson learnt-check 'em in and check 'em out.

More importantly, we were reminded how lucky we were. In conversation with a member of the hotel staff team, we chatted about Kruger, it was literally over the fence at the bottom of the garden. This lady was in her forties and had never been to Kruger. For us, it was just our next destination on a year of wandering, for her visiting the park was the stuff of dreams. How lucky we were and how important it was not to take the opportunities we had for granted. We decided she was welcome to the missing laundry.

Kruger National Park is a wildlife paradise, covering an area the size of Wales. The Welsh tend to love it when we use their country as some sort of international ruler. The park is home to 32,000 zebra, 25,000 buffalo, 17,000 wildebeest, 12,000 elephants, 9,000 giraffes, 5,000 white rhinos, 1,500 lions, 1,000 shy leopards and just 200 cheetahs. And a partridge in a pear tree. We knew we would have to be extremely lucky to see leopard or cheetah. But that was our aim, cheetah for Roonagh and Spotty, and leopard to complete the Big Five.

We saw at least one of all the above, except for the reclusive leopard. Five glorious days were spent in Kruger, staying at two camps. Firstly, in a rondavel, a traditional round hut, and then a tent on stilts next to a dried-out riverbed where elephants stomped past at night and hyenas howled in the distance.

Across the five days, the first five hours were the best in terms of animal spotting. Here are the highlights.

Forty-five minutes surrounded by a pride of lions. For the avoidance of doubt, we were in a car.

Two herds of elephants, about 50 beasts in total, crossing the road directly in front of us. I had to reverse very quickly as they came straight through where we were parked up. Fortunately, elephants have poor eyesight.

A couple of memorable night drives where we saw more lion, hyena, white-tailed mongoose, spotted genet and black-backed jackal.

I also did a dawn bushwalk. Me, two friendly men and a pair of large guns. No Big Five, but we did stumble across the remains of an elephant carcass and a giraffe's skull. Dead animals were not really what I was looking for, but it was great to get away from the roads and appreciate Kruger's wilderness.

We left Kruger exhilarated but exhausted. Our next destination was only an hour away, the geological stunner which is the Blyde River Canyon. At 26 kilometres in length, this is the third-largest canyon on the planet. Its colours were very different from the world's largest canyon, the Grand Canyon. Rather than the latter's deep shades of brown, orange and yellow, Blyde was surrounded by sub-tropical vegetation.

We enjoyed another river boat cruise, admiring the distinctive rock formations, laughing at some of the descriptions of shapes offered by the pre-recorded audio guide and making up our own cloud shapes.

"That rock looks like a donkey. That cloud looks like a trout. That bridge looks like a badger."

Apart from a boat trip, we spent three days chilling and recharging our batteries. Blyde was out of season and dead quiet. We had almost exclusive use of the heated outdoor pool on our campsite. The weather was pleasant, and we enjoyed updating diaries, editing photos, playing putt-putt (crazy golf), wee walks and trips to the campsite shop. The grounds were full of marauding kudu, bushbuck and many monkeys.

Travelling on a budget can test your morals, and on at least one occasion, we fell short. One afternoon we heard a loud crash inside our chalet. The terrifying sound of shattered glass flying through the air, like a scene from *The Omen*. Followed by the screams of children.

Rory had somehow managed to fall off a chair and propel himself headfirst through a large window. Thankfully, he was unscathed despite the dramatic nature of his fall. Fearful of the hefty repair bill, we scooped up the glass, put it back inside the room and reported the attempted burglary to the park reception.

"Someone must have attempted to break into the chalet because the window was broken" I tentatively proffered to the stern-faced receptionist.

We got away with this deceit but what a dreadful example to set to our children. We should be sent to the naughty step for parents.

At the time, I was reading Sir Bobby Charlton's autobiography. The legendary England and Manchester United footballer shared the experience of sharing a room with Nobby Stiles, a fearless, toothless and notoriously clumsy man. Nobby would fall over on any occasion and drop things with reckless abandon. Our Rory soon became known as *Nobby* and would fall over many times during our travels. Fortunately, he never did himself serious harm, always bouncing like a rubber ball.

One month in, eleven to go. If truth be told, we were still in holiday mode. That sensation would dissipate as the weeks passed, but for now, this was simply the best family holiday we had ever experienced. We had gone through a period of adjustment and were becoming more relaxed as time went by. Every day was a new adventure and we rarely heard the immortal childhood phrase "I'm bored."

Fitting everything in was the challenge. In all honesty, you can't, so it's better to enjoy the moment and not fret about what you might miss. Kruger certainly taught us that. Game spotting can become addictive, especially when you're trying to bag that flipping leopard.

We always knew that South Africa would feel like the holiday of a lifetime before we started travelling for real. Everything was booked in advance, and we had the luxury of a car. So far, it was easy. This was about to change. After a short stop in Johannesburg, it would be Mauritius, Madagascar, Mauritius again, Johannesburg again, Hong Kong and China within a month. Watch out world, Family Trippers were on their way.

Madagascar
Windy pops and bananas

Our 11 day trip to the Red Island, so-called because the ground is bright red, like terracotta roofs in Italy, saw us staying in seven different accommodations of a wide-ranging standard. The food ranged from bland to inedible, especially given we were restricted to the vegetarian options. Road distances were huge and we spent many long hours in the car.

And it was worth it all, many times over. A fantastic visit to this special place time nearly forgot.

What can I tell you about Madagascar? There are lemurs, of course, our main reason for coming here. More of these wee chaps later. The island looks nothing like its fictional incarnation in the DreamWorks movie, but that's Hollywood for you.

Madagascar is the world's fourth-largest island. Go to Wikipedia if you are desperate to know the other three. Being a former colony of France, French is widely spoken, although the primary language is Malagasy. It is one of the world's poorer nations. We saw many heart-rending scenes as we drove around the island. Overpopulation is a massive problem, increasing at 3% per annum, with 45% of Malagasy being under 14 years of age. So is deforestation, the devastation of virgin rainforest for palm oil production leading to the distinctive red soil bleeding into the rivers and sea.

Education is neither compulsory nor free and from what we saw, most kids, from an early age, either work in the fields or beg in the streets. The people seemed friendly and resilient, with a ready smile and low crime levels, and we experienced much kindness. The economy is subsistence-based with few exports, although half the world's vanilla supply originates in Madagascar. A tribal system still exists, with half the population practising traditional beliefs. The other half are Christian.

All good travellers understand that serendipity is an essential ingredient of a successful journey. You may recall, prior to the trip, I spent three months volunteering in Sri Lanka. One night, in a bar in Kandy, I got chatting with a British travel journalist. Inevitably we soon began talking about my upcoming adventure. I guess I was telling anybody and everybody about it at the time, whether they wanted to listen or not. I mentioned Madagascar was on our itinerary, and he said, "Oh, my sister is married to a guy from Madagascar. If you need any help arranging things let me know."

I took his details, and through him, we were able to arrange a driver to take us around the island. What a stroke of luck.

We arrived excited and nervous at the dusty and sleepy Madagascar International Airport. We had arranged for our driver Hajalala to meet us ahead of our first night in the capital city Antananarivo, *Tana* for short. We passed through arrivals on time to find he was not there.

"Oh my God" I said to Anne, out of earshot of the kids who were blissfully unaware of my growing anxiety.

"We've been ripped off. He's not going to turn up. This is a scam. What are we going to do?"

Suddenly we were outside our comfort zone, and the realities of travel started to dawn. Of course, my concerns were utter rubbish. He was simply slightly delayed and soon appeared in the arrival hall, smiling and delighted to see us. We were in the developing world after all. Why would timekeeping be of the same standard as we were accustomed to in the UK? We were beginning to learn that life isn't ruled by the clock everywhere in the world.

Out we went to the car, ever so slightly worried about what we might find. A wreck presumably. After all, this was a scam conceived in a bar in Sri Lanka six months previously.

"How gullible am I, the inexperienced traveller no longer on vacation."

The paranoid thoughts of a man out of his comfort zone. For there in the car park was a brand-new Toyota Land Cruiser, our luxury chariot for our adventures ahead.

It soon transpired that Hajalala was not our driver. He was an entrepreneur who owned the Land Cruiser and employed drivers to take tourists around the island. The next day we were introduced to our driver Thomas, a cheery, rotund and swarthy fellow. We got on well with him. That French I had learnt all those years ago at University finally came into its own. I didn't care whether I sounded like Inspector Clouseau. Thomas and I had many hours to spend together as driver and front-seat passenger, so we chatted away, me digging deep to retrieve my French from the far recesses of my memory.

Thomas took great care of the vehicle. No doubt it was part of his job description. Every time we stopped for a visit at an attraction or eatery, he would bring out a cloth, spit on it and give the bodywork a good polish. Unless we were mistaken, he also had a lady friend in every town. Just a hunch, but we were pretty sure we were right, based on how quickly he dropped us off at every new destination. I hope these days he has shares in Tinder. He might even have invented it.

Three hours east of Tana, our first stop was Andasibe, the only place in the world where the largest lemur, the Indri-Indri live. Indri grow to 60 centimetres in length, with a rudimentary tail, large hands and massive feet. Their round head has a pointed face and circular furry ears. They have a very distinctive call which sounds like a cross between a fire engine and an opera singer in pain. Described in guidebooks as looking like "*a four-year-old child in a panda suit*," the Indri are endangered, with only 1,000 animals remaining. They do not survive in captivity or breeding programmes as, when captured, they refuse to eat and die. How tragic is that.

We were led on a four-hour sweaty trek through the humid jungle reserve looking for Indri. Eventually, the fire engine sounded its siren, the fat lady started to sing, and we heard their distinctive call. We found a conspiracy of lemurs, *conspiracy* being the collective noun for lemurs. Rory asked me why they had that name? Great question, who knows, maybe in the past lemurs have carried out heists or organised revolutions.

Perched high in the branches of a leafy tree was a large female nursing her six week old baby. I was so pleased the children were lucky enough to see this unique animal in its natural habitat. We stood looking up at mother and child for several minutes, amazed at our good fortune. Sadly, the tranquillity of this special moment was ruined by a group of Italian tourists who seemed to think they were at a Milan derby football match or a Bruce Springsteen concert in the San Siro.

We spent our first two nights in a dank and dark chalet within striking distance of the Reserve. We were the Indri's next-door neighbours. The grounds were resplendent with giant poinsettias, their distinctive red flowers reaching for the sun through the forest dawn's low hanging mist, their sweet-scented aroma permeating the tropical air. These were not the Poinsettias that sit on dining room tables at Christmas, but massive and dramatic bushes befitting Madagascar's national flower.

Brown lemurs charged around the grounds, the local equivalent of squirrels we might see in the woods back home. As if this wasn't enough for an 8 and 10 year old, and a 40 year old kid, there was a mini-gym where they enjoyed, and their Dad endured, an extensive daily workout regime. In my defence, during my volunteering experience in Sri Lanka earlier that year, I had fallen ill with an infection. I was hospitalised and lost a stone in weight, which I scarcely had to lose in the first place. But compared to the locals, I was positively obese, as we were about to discover.

The main tourist route in Madagascar, the Route du Sud, heads south from Tana. Our first stop was a night in Antsirabe where we saw extreme poverty which was deeply upsetting. A real dilemma was whether to give loose change to child beggars and pleading mothers with babies in their arms. Their appeals were too heart-wrenching to resist and we acceded, partial redemption for our inaction in Swaziland.

The town's fragile economy appeared to be based on the rickshaw industry. Known as *pousse-pousse*, these wooden carts were propelled by skinny men with gaunt features, whip-thin legs and bare feet. A full set of teeth could not be found in any of their imploring faces as they touted for business outside our hotel. We were relentlessly pursued everywhere we went.

Thomas insisted we spend an hour being transported in a couple of these colourful chariots, like Roman emperors processing to the Colosseum. Initially reluctant to submit to such exploitative behaviours, we eventually conceded to avoid being culturally insensitive and hurting feelings. We also realised that our two dollar fare would put food on the table for our driver's family that evening. We were relieved the tour proceeded at walking pace. Our shabby yet surprisingly strong charioteers didn't run for tourists at the same speed they did for their regular local passengers.

Thomas also insisted we visit a gemstone museum.

"Mr Ian, there are tortoises for your children to see."

Once again, we were reluctant and with good reason. There was a clear expectation that these wealthy westerners would spend a fistful of dollars in the gift shop. No way Jose, or Thomas in our case, much to his scarcely masked chagrin. No doubt, he was looking forward to his commission.

There was no way we were purchasing overpriced jewellery. We spent as short a time in the museum as we could get reasonably get away with, beat a hasty retreat and a few days later presented the free gemstones they had insisted we take as a gift to grateful local children.

The following day our trusty Land Cruiser took us six hours down the Route du Sud to the Ranomafana Rainforest, with both kids throwing up into makeshift sick bags on the back seat.

"Don't take anti-malarial drugs on an empty stomach kids."

We stopped on the way to extract hard currency from an ATM in a dusty town, a nervous Thomas standing guard nearby in case of bandits. I am pleased to report no bandits appeared. I am not sure if Thomas was being over-protective or just winding me up.

We then had a coffee stop where we nearly lost a child. Not for the last time. The café's resident Alsatian was on a longer leash than we anticipated, charged forward teeth bared and came within an inch of taking Roonagh's face off. What a good job she was an innocent animal lover. I was quaking in my boots, the incident triggering my lifelong fear of dogs having been chased by the same breed as a young child. To this day, Anne has no memory of the event, the protective memory of a terrified mother suppressing the reality of this potentially life-changing incident.

We arrived mid-afternoon at our rustic hotel, perched on a hillside overlooking a ramshackle town. Wood-burning stoves powered everything- heating, cooking and hot water. The humid air hung heavy with charcoal-infused smoke. We had some emergency clothes washing to do. The clothes started dry and dirty and ended up damp and pungent.

When darkness fell, we walked along the road to the nearest pizzeria. Believe me, Malagasy pizza is like nothing on earth, especially not pizza and not in a good way. Imagine coming home drunk one night, getting a supermarket pizza out of the freezer, putting it in the oven and then eating the cardboard packaging while you wait. It was a bit like that.

On the way back to the hotel, I fell victim to one of the curses of the developing world, a lack of street lighting. To the amusement of the rest of the family, I fell into a hole at the side of the road, disappearing quickly from view, like a snowman on a sunny day. I suffered no ill-effects, but it was obvious from where young *Nobby* acquired his talent.

In Madagascar, Roonagh experienced what we frivolously called *"windy pops,"* less attractively known as trapped wind. Except we didn't know that's what it was at the time. Our first thought was appendicitis. The poor girl was in so much pain, screaming and yelping, clutching her stomach and in floods of tears. This lasted for an hour and a half. Remember we were in the middle of nowhere. The nearest hospital was hours away and who knows what standard it would be.

Eventually, Anne said, "I am just going to give her a heartburn tablet to see if that helps. It's a long shot but worth a try."

Sure enough, this did the trick. After a hilarious hour of involuntary burping, the "windy pops" passed, and we resumed the day's activities safe in the knowledge that all was well.

One evening we had an unexpected shock. Whilst getting ready for bed, Anne exclaimed, "Oh shoot, I have missed a pill. I've got an extra one." "Shoot." wasn't the actual expletive she used.

Anne worked out she had messed up her routine with her contraceptive pill due to time differences and flights. Imagine what went through our minds. Not only were we happy with the two trippers we had, but an unexpected pregnancy would have had a dramatic impact on the remaining 11 months of our trip. At the risk of a spoiler, this proved to be a false alarm.

The next morning the sun was shining, and Thomas suggested we visit the local thermal swimming pool. It was less swimming pool, more communal bathtub, jam packed with locals cleaning themselves as they splashed around. We fancied a dip, even though we knew that Thomas was solely motivated by the inevitable commission.

The ever-vigilant Anne took one look at the disease-infested pool and uttered the wise words, "I don't think so."

But too late as we three kids jumped in. For about 30 seconds. It was filthy. Not to mention the fur balls of human hair floating in the putrid water.

Standing at the side of the pool, Anne grimaced and yelled, "Everybody out!"

When I explained what had happened to Thomas, he replied, "Oh, today is Monday. The pool is cleaned weekly on a Wednesday." He could have mentioned that before.

We woke early the next day for a four hour lemur walk in the rainforest. The sun had disappeared, and it never came back. It rains 260 days a year, and we shouldn't have expected anything else. At least we missed one of the six cyclones they had already experienced that year.

On our muddy, wet walk we were fortunate with our lemur sightings. Especially because we saw a pair of Broad Nosed Greater Bamboo Lemurs. Weighing in at 2.5 kilograms and reaching 50 centimetres in length, these critically endangered lemurs feed almost exclusively on one particular bamboo species which contains enough cyanide to kill a human. Fortunately, they are immune to such toxins.

At dusk, we went back to the rainforest and stood in a clearing where we saw Fossa, a cat-like carnivorous mammal and the lemur's main predator. We had all heard of Fossa, they feature in the DreamWorks movie.

Lastly, we found the world's smallest primate, the diminutive mouse lemur. Malagasy people have traditionally associated these primates with spirits because they are active at night and have an eerie, large-eyed stare. For us, they were just adorably cute. We deduced that the guides laid food on the ground to entice these animals and it was a bit of a touristy experience, with mandatory noisy Italians thrown in for good measure. However, it was still better than seeing these animals in a zoo. They were in the wild, and yes, that is a *Madagascar* movie reference.

The rainforests of Madagascar were also full of chameleons. Half of all the world's 150 species live here. Funnily enough, they were not always easy to spot. The Leaf chameleon, for example, looked like a leaf. The Pygmy chameleon was very small, the size of a fingertip. Others were large and colourful, such as the bright green Parson's chameleon and the multi-coloured Panther chameleon, who strutted about looking like Joseph in his *Amazing* Technicoloured Dreamcoat.

With clothes as wet and muddy as the rainforest itself, we drove another three hours south to the beautiful highland town of Ambalavao. This charismatic place was how we envisaged South America would be in a few months' time, set at altitude, with mountains affording sweeping vistas. The locals wore colourful woollen blankets and straw hats. The women carried bundles of firewood and wicker baskets of vegetables on their heads on their way to and from the bustling market. Others sat on their haunches, with their home-grown produce spread out across the dusty ground or on a threadbare blanket. Frequently they only had one product line, such as tomatoes or potatoes.

Men chatted walking along streets framed by bougainvillaea adorned walls. They carried their lives in their faces as they chewed tobacco, leaned on street corners and played cards with each other. It was humbling to see people appearing so old and wizened, realising they may well be younger than the 40 year old me.

We arrived during the noisy weekly zebu market, framed against a backdrop of forests and grey mountains. The air crackled with the sound of auctions and arguments, set to a soundtrack of agitated animals objecting to their imminent fate.

Zebu is a breed of cattle which symbolises wealth in Madagascan society. A large specimen fetches 250 Euros at auction. They are used as bovine tractors in the field as well for their meat. However, they have a low milk yield, just four litres per day.

In a rather curious tradition, before a man marries, he must steal a zebu to prove his manhood. If caught, the punishment is five months in prison, or much worse if the owner hunts you down.

The main reason for our trip to Ambalavao was to visit Parc d'Anja, home to a colony of 200 ring-tailed lemurs. Adrien, a local conservationist, started the reserve ten years previously. This colony would have been eradicated by locals hunting them for food, were it not for Adrien's efforts. He persuaded them to turn to other forms of sustainable agriculture, protect the lemurs, and transform the reserve into a tourist attraction. As a result, the villagers are more economically secure, and the lemur colony is safe and thriving. A win-win.

Thomas had used his influence and secured Adrien as our guide for the day. He was brilliant, especially with the kids. The reserve sits in the most beautiful of settings: mountains, paddy fields, huge boulders and forest. Our new favourite place on the planet. Lemurs were everywhere we turned. Just for the kids, Adrien brought along some bananas to hand feed lemurs. To be able to hold hands with these animals and feel their soft fur was a real privilege. They were adorable.

To top it all off, as a special treat for the kids, Adrien took us back for a couple of hours at sunset when the park was closed. It was true what other family travellers had told us, having kids with you opens doors which are otherwise closed. We clambered up some precarious rocks, free from the constraints of health and safety risk assessments and sat with two groups of lemurs as they bedded down for the night on a sun-kissed rock. Day 45 of the trip was, we all agreed, the best so far.

Diary Extract: Rory, age 10

Today was rock climbing, lemur feeding and zebu patting day. For we were going on a tour of the zebu market and the Anja Reserve. Thomas had found us simply the best guide because our guide created the Anja Reserve.

So the first thing we did on the tour was a half hour walk around the zebu market. Zebus are a mix between a cow and a camel which were originally found in India. We were allowed to pat someone's zebu on its squidgy hump.

After the zebu market we set off to the Anja Reserve where we had almost a hundred percent chance of seeing a ring-tailed lemur. It only took two minutes to find about 20 hungry rtls sun-bathing on a rock so we decided to join them on the rock. We stayed with this lot of rtls for about 3/4 of an hour and everyone fed them except me because it was bananas we feed them. Before we climbed some of the rocks of the reserve we bumped into about 10 more groups of rtls. When we did some rock climbing at the reserve we got the most spectacular views of the Madagascar landscape. Soon after the good bit of rock climbing, we spotted the biggest chameleon of all, the panther chameleon. Also nearby was some more rtls, some sleeping, some playing. On our way back we only saw a leaf chameleon which is called that because its tail looks just like a dead leaf.

Then Adrien took us to the small paper factory which is in the grounds of the hotel. Then Adrien offered to take us back to the reserve for free at 4 so we said ok, of course. After all that it was lunch time so Mum and Dad bought some baguette for lunch. After lunch we made friends with 3 kids and gave them a ball and some gemstones and we ended up playing with them all afternoon.

Then we went back to Anja and, you know what, it only took 2 minutes to find the rtls. Then we did some of the most extreme rock climbing. After a bit of rock climbing we reached the end of that part of the trail. On top of that you could see the most extraordinary scene of the lemurs bedding down for the night with a strange background of Mexican dusk, weird. Then we did some more life threatening climbing.

Then it was getting dark so we had to leave the stunning Anja reserve. Then I had a crepe au fromage for tea at the hotel. Then it was time for the tired trippers to get back to the bungalow with their thoughts full of lemurs."

Diary Extract: Roonagh, age 8

Today I have a big day! First we saw the zebu market for half an hour. Then the excitement starts. We head up to Anja Reserve but before that we have to buy some bananas to feed the ring-tailed lemurs! I was very excited when I first saw the lemurs very high in a tree! But I was wrong because we saw them on the rock right next to me and their little hands pulling my hand to their tiny little mouths to get the bananas! And their tails were so soft! Then we climbed up the rock and I almost fell.

Then we went back and looked at the paper factory and saw how they make paper for 10 minutes. I was thrilled when Adrien (tour guide) told us that we could meet him at 4.00 at the Anja Reserve to see the cute little lemurs all cuddled up on the rock and to feed them and with no other people shouting and screaming.

First we had a baguette for lunch. After that we sorted our photos and then put them on the laptop and gave some little boys behind a fence that separated the hotel and their houses some gifts like balls and gemstones that we did not need anymore. Then we went to the shop for 5 mins and then we went to the market for, oh I don't know, about half an hour.

Then time for the ANJA RESERVE. Wahooooo! Time to see my old friends again (the ring-tailed lemurs). Yey. I'm looking forward to this!

Right then, time to get back to Anja. First, yep, Mr Greedy Guts ate a whole banana already (a greedy ring-tailed lemur!). After that we went off to try and find some more lemurs to feed but not that same lemur! Once we had found some more lemurs one of them bit my finger! And nearly stood on my toe, WHAT A CHEEKY LEMUR!

After that we went back climbing, dun dun dun...! But first it's the easy bit but luckily we stopped before the hard bit to see the lemurs sleeping and climbing and guess what they sat on my knee when I was feeding them! Then we did the hard part. Oh gosh, I can't dare to think about it.

The two day, 500 kilometres journey back to Tana awaited us. We experienced our worst night yet at the Green Park Hotel back in Antsirabe. Thomas was insistent we stop again in this unremarkable town. I suspect one of his lady friends had unfinished business.

Our beds were more plywood than mattress, the pillows more sacks of potatoes than fluffy feather bundles. After a sleepless night, we attempted to wash off the night-time sweat under a few drops of cold water, with a bin liner as a shower curtain, surrounded by exposed electrical wires.

Surviving intact, we made it back to Tana in time for a Saturday afternoon of retail therapy. We had a reservation for the popular Hotel Sakamanga, popular with western visitors. However, we were disappointed to discover that the Wi-Fi wasn't working. On such small details are treats on the road made or broken. All hope of uploading our blogs, photos, emailing friends and researching accommodation for the next month vanished. We shopped instead and then gorged ourselves on Mexican Pizza, Madagascan style. Just this once we were not ashamed.

Anne and I concluded the evening with a drink in the hotel bar. They had wine on the menu, and we fancied a rare treat. We placed our order and waited patiently as the barman gestured to his friend, hiding in the corner like an indigenous chameleon. The invisible man disappeared, returning 20 minutes later with a bottle of Jacob's Creek in a 7/11 carrier bag, clearly procured from a local corner store at a substantially lower price than the £20 these gullible tourists were happy to pay.

We toasted the end of our time in Madagascar, a country with which we now had a real affinity. We wished we had more time to explore the island. A visit every year for the next 20 would provide completely different experiences. We knew when we returned to real life, Madagascar would feel like a dream. We hope when our kids are parents, they bring their children to see the Indri-Indri and ring-tailed lemurs. With a bit of luck and a lot of conservation, these remarkable creatures will still be there.

Mauritius
It's no honeymoon

To Mauritius. Romantic island nestled in the Indian Ocean. Paradise for honeymooners. A last-minute addition to our flight itinerary and our jumping-off point for Madagascar.

We visited Mauritius twice. Before Madagascar and again afterwards. Both visits sandwiched between city stops in Johannesburg.

There were times when we just needed a break from what some people would erroneously think was a holiday. A holiday from the holiday. Travelling can be tiring as well as exhilarating. To be truthful, exhilarating can be exhausting when it just keeps coming. We had 100 days during our year away which will stay with us forever. The most amazing, unforgettable and awe-inspiring days. But the other 250 were just as important. Playing with the kids, hanging out, chatting to locals and other travellers. Then there was planning to do, blogs to write, calls back home, shopping and clothes to wash. There is a saying that

It's the interruptions which make the journey worthwhile. So true, family time was the raison d'etre of this adventure after all.

Over the year our average length of accommodation stay was 3.5 nights. That's a bucket load full of moving about, packing and unpacking and many different beds of highly variable quality. We didn't want travel to be so relentless that we lost the fun and pleasure. Mauritius was the perfect opportunity to rest up for a few days either side of our adventures in Madagascar.

Relax is precisely what we did in Mauritius. Not in a romantic all-inclusive holiday resort. Oh no, that was not who we were and why we were there.

This was in the days before Airbnb so finding a suitable place to stay online was not easy. Eventually, I found a listing for a Scottish run family guesthouse in the small resort town of Trou aux Biches.

Free and widely available Wi-Fi was not yet a thing. Uploading a month's worth of photos racked up a bill of £150. Quite a budget hit but one we had to take. Imagine losing a month's photos, what a calamity that would be. More on this later.

When I tell you that the highlights from this leg included the hotel's resident Dalmatian, a dog called "*Donald*," and the unnamed tortoise in the front garden, you will start to get an idea of how busy we weren't. But the guest house was five minutes' walk from a beautiful tropical beach, and the local bar was the first opportunity we had to watch some of the Beijing Summer Olympics. More on that later.

Like Madagascar, Mauritius is an island in the Indian Ocean off Africa's coast with a French colonial past. But that is where the similarities end. Mauritius, or to use its proper moniker *Ile de Maurice*, was not backpacker friendly. Only the capital, Port Louis, had an authentic feel to it. High-end resorts predominately populated the beach-fringed coastline. Designer shops, yachts and cocktails. Touts on the beach, ridiculous prices and miles of wobbly white European bellies.

One evening we fancied seeing an advertised display of traditional local dancing on the beach. Authentic culture, of course. Not. The performance was purely for tourists. But it was free. So long as you sat in the beachside bar of a five-star resort. We arrived early and perused the menu. One round of drinks would have blown a day's budget. Rather sheepishly we ordered one large bottle of water and four glasses. For five dollars. Ouch. The dancing was good enough, although not as memorable as we would see later in Asia and South America. But good enough value for a fiver.

In the outside food court of a waterside shopping mall in Port Louis, I finally plucked up the courage to break the tragic news to Roonagh that her cat back home was missing in action. As you may recall, Hattie had bolted over a neighbour's hedge when we delivered her for safekeeping just before we left home. My vain and lingering hope she might suddenly reappear at their doorstep one day was clearly not to be fulfilled.

"Roonagh, I have some news. Some sad news. I am afraid that Hattie will not be at home when we get back."

I explained what had happened. Cue a bucket load of snot and tears. I forget what bribery I had to use to stem the flood. It probably included ice cream and coke (liquid, not powder), but at least the news was off my chest.

In hindsight, there were two animal activities that we wish we had not bothered with.

Firstly, a trip on a catamaran. A beautiful boat on a gorgeous day, floating on the Indian Ocean under a bright blue sky. We joined a flotilla of dolphin seekers. Every time one skipper spotted a dolphin, every other vessel revved its engine and charged in hot pursuit towards the poor animals. With obvious results. Being budget trippers, ours was the oldest craft, so each time we arrived there were no dolphins left to see. They had fled as quickly as they could at the sound of intruders.

We also visited a Tortoise Park. Giant tortoises of the same genus as those in the Galápagos Islands we anticipated seeing later in our travels. The kids had a piggyback ride on these massive animals. I am not sure it was the best thing from an animal rights point of view. Maybe we should have taken the opportunity instead to explain the ethical considerations to our impressionable young companions. Parents make mistakes though. It happens, so let's move on.

Beyond this, there was not too much to report. These were a pleasant and functional couple of stopovers, nothing more.

As our early morning taxi sped towards the airport for our flight back to mainland Africa for the last time, we reflected how fortunate we were. Along with hanging on for dear life as our taxi careered around every corner, Anne nudging the driver awake as his eyelids drooped.

It was a good visit but not a great one. As neither of us plans to marry again, we are unlikely to return to the honeymoon island of Mauritius.

South Africa
Déjà vu again

Two visits, two very different impressions of Johannesburg, the City of Gold. One of the unwritten rules of travel is that no two stays are the same. How you feel about a place can be transformed by the weather, the political climate or your mood at the time. Whether or not you have kids with you may well be a factor as well, although we never had the opportunity to test that premise during our year together.

Visit one saw us based in a white residential suburb called Linden. Our base was much further out than we had anticipated, and we didn't go downtown on that occasion.

Our overall impression of this area was white middle-class families in big houses behind tall gates and intricate security systems. We heard a lot about high crime levels and a fear of what was happening in post-apartheid South Africa.

One evening we hailed a taxi to collect a takeaway, our first ever Nando's. Next to the restaurant was an ATM.

Our driver calmly said, "There was an armed robbery here a couple of hours ago. A guy got shot really bad. I hear he was killed."

We were given the very sage advice not to drive at night. "If you do, always have your doors locked and go straight through red lights rather than stopping at them."

Fortunately, night-time driving was not necessary during our time in South Africa. It was, however, where I got the first of three speeding tickets during our year. The other two were in Australia, including me breaking the speed limit in a camper-van. In South Africa, the financial penalty is based on how fast you are going. The greater the percentage over the official speed limit, the higher the fine. I must have been going fast because the damage was two days' budget.

"Sir, you can pay me 600 Rand in cash now, or you can jump in the back of my patrol car and pay at the station. Which would you prefer Sir?"

600 Rand was about £150. I coughed up there and then, no doubt at a premium which never reached the Government. With two kids in the back, I did not mind.

On our second visit, we organised a tour with the taxi driver who had taken us to the airport at the end of our first stay. Much cheaper than an organised tour and way more flexible. As we went around the world, we often found hiring a local cabbie more affordable and authentic than tour agencies. This was one of the many travel lessons I learnt in Sri Lanka.

Our driver took us on a memorable and evocative tour of Soweto, a place I had heard so much about as the hotbed of black resistance during the apartheid era. We probably didn't go to the most impoverished parts for safety reasons. We explored

Orlando, home of the Mandelas, Tutus and Sisulus in the bad years. How it had changed. There had been massive regeneration. The housing quality was much better than I had witnessed just five years previously in the townships. This was encouraging, although there was clearly a long way to go. Maybe my perceptions were altered by the contrast with the extreme poverty we had just witnessed in Madagascar. Soweto was positively middle class in comparison.

A visit to the excellent Apartheid Museum was also a powerful and poignant reminder of just how far things had progressed, despite the problems of poverty, crime and disease. Especially tear-jerking was our stop at the Hector Pietersen Museum in Orlando. On 16 June 1976, several thousand school kids took part in a peaceful march to protest at being forced to learn Afrikaans as their first language. Hector Pietersen was the first to be shot as police opened fire and killed 600 children. Horrific and a turning point in the struggle.

As we prepared to leave for Asia's tropical climate, it was time to reduce our burgeoning luggage. We had already dispatched home our first parcel of goodies from Mauritius. Not just mementoes purchased in Africa, but also many things we had brought from home and now realised we did not need or had no room for in our backpacks. Some clothes would be pointless in Asia's heat and humidity, so we donated jackets, jeans and jumpers to the grateful housekeeper at our guesthouse. Another bookend to the donation of those football shirts in Cape Town two months previously, as the first two months of our year away came to a close.

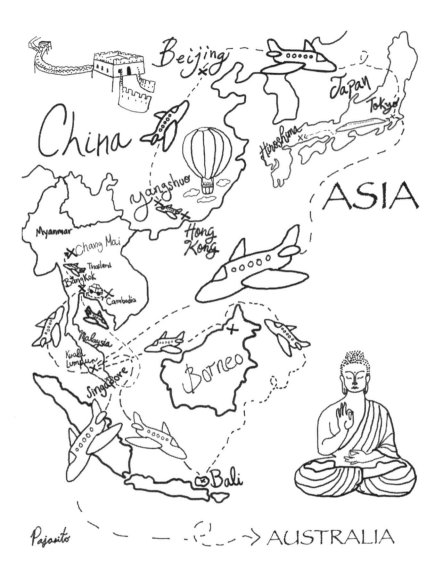

Hong Kong
Will Spotty survive?

Hong Kong. Air pollution, sea pollution, light pollution. Home to 7.5 million people. Beautiful, vibrant and fun. This former British colony, and Special Administrative Region of the People's Republic of China, provided a gentle launchpad for month three of our travels, a trip through the *Far East*. Welcome to Manhattan, Asian style.

First things first, Hong Kong is not an island. It is an archipelago scattered off the mainland peninsula of Kowloon. A cluster of islands, 261 in total. Hong Kong Island itself is at the heart of things and was our base for a four-night stopover.

The Special Administrative Region was a former British Colony slowly adjusting to life in new ownership. We saw no evidence of the political and security difficulties which would emerge a decade later. Perhaps grievances and dissatisfaction were bubbling under the surface, at a level invisible to an innocent traveller. But for us, this visit was about seeing some sights and having a gentle entry into the three month Asian leg of our travels.

Early impressions were that Hong Kong was cosmopolitan, westernised and dripping with money. We had never seen so many designer shops anywhere. The brand was everywhere, there was even a Marks & Spencer's food hall.

Before the trip, I had used discount vouchers from our grocery shopping to purchase a lifetime membership of the International Youth Hostelling Association. Subscription entitled us to a 10% discount off youth hostels worldwide. I figured hostels would be the mainstay of our travels. How wrong I was. Our first experience would end up being our last.

We had booked into the Jockey Club Mt Davis Hostel for our four nights in Hong Kong. This proved to be a rookie error. Tripper lesson - after a long overnight flight, in this case 13 hours from Johannesburg, book a top-notch hotel. Preferably in a central location.

The Hostel was 30 minutes away from the action downtown and only accessible by an infrequent shuttle bus service, but that was the least of our problems. To be fair, it did have a dramatic location perched atop a hill, cocooned above the omnipresent smog in a blanket of humidity. The problem was the rooms. Think of a prison. But a very basic prison. In 35 degrees heat and 85% humidity. At night.

We had two bunk beds in one small room. No windows, no electricity, no air. The mattresses would have been shiny white vinyl, like the cover of a cheap 1970s sofa, were it not for layers of darkened mould camouflaging the slippery surface with a mottled patchwork of black and green splodges. Our only friends were the colony of cockroaches who scuttled to and fro across the harsh concrete floor. Even with the exhaustion of a night-time flight, sleep was not our friend.

We emerged into the early morning heat, destroyed and bereft of energy.

Anne said, "I know this wasn't meant to be a holiday, but we really are taking it to the next level now."

I took this as a call to action, from wife to husband, from mother to father, from mama tripper to papa tripper.

The one saving grace of this penal institution was that it had Wi-Fi. A scarce and precious commodity for backpackers in the less connected world of 2008. I retrieved the laptop from my prison cell, perched at an outdoor table overlooking the metropolis below, mopped my perspiring brow and started googling. Fortunately, travel websites had been invented, and hotels were using them to sell vacant rooms at affordable prices. However, family rooms were not easy to find in the Far East. I don't know if this is because of the small size of families. We experienced the same challenge when researching accommodation options for both Japan and China. We had to go upmarket. For once the budget could go on its own trip.

Later that morning, we checked into our suite in a five-star hotel for three nights of sheer bliss. We had a gym, 25-metre rooftop pool and an onsite restaurant with buffet breakfast. We had carpet, Wi-Fi, and cable TV. Slippers, dressing gowns and air conditioning. And the most fantastic view out across the Bay. Heaven. This is how tripping should be. Not really, but we learnt that occasionally a treat went a long way in boosting morale and reducing homesickness.

Our three full days in Hong Kong flew by. Limited time and jet lag meant we could not do everything we wanted. Another tripper lesson: three or four days would be sufficient for two adults, but a full week would be about right for a family. We applied this learning wherever we could for the remainder of our year away as we visited other metropolises. Go slower, see more.

Taking the tram up the near-vertical ascent to Victoria Peak, the highest point in Hong Kong, we observed local tourists engaged in the bizarre practice of having models of their hands crafted by dipping them in vats of hot wax. These strange events took place at the front of a shopping centre. I did not dare venture inside for fear of what alternative body parts might be being wax dipped in the deeper recesses of this enterprise.

We spent an evening on the *Avenue of Stars* by the harbourside, which felt like New York City would be if they moved Times Square down to the Hudson River. Much like Hollywood Boulevard, movie stars leave imprints of their hands in the pavement, although Jackie Chan's was the only one we recognised. At 8.00 pm every night there was an amazing, and more importantly, free lights show in the harbour.

Lantau Island is home to the world's largest outdoor seated Buddha. Not the only Buddha statue we visited in the world claiming this particular title. A ferry ride was followed by a 20 minute vertigo-inducing cable car ride offering tremendous views of the entire Hong Kong archipelago.

At the island's peak sits a Buddha theme village, chock-a-block with tourist shops, takeaways and touts. More in keeping with the island's religious purpose, we found a Monastery with a vast vegetarian canteen where we were served a wide range of obscure, indescribable and, at times, inedible food items. More accurately, the parents had lunch and the kids pushed some stuff around their plates.

The post-lunch climb up the 268 steps to the Buddha was challenging in 33 degrees heat and 86% humidity. However, we achieved our mission, and the views made it all worthwhile. One small step to Nirvana.

We took a few rides across the boat-studded harbour, heaving with local ferries and traditional junks. The packed Star Ferry from Hong Kong Island to Kowloon was well worth the 12p fare.

The final highlight was found in our decadent hotel itself. Shortly before our departure to China, we indulged in an *all you can eat* Sunday lunch buffet. We gorged ourselves on unusual concoctions such as red bean ice cream through to salads peppered with succulent Stilton Cheese from back home. I must confess, at the point the latter tickled my tastebuds, the tantalising sensation brought a tear or two to my eyes. Remember by this point I had been out of the UK for almost six months, including my Sri Lanka adventure. Home comforts were by now sorely missed.

Eventually, we could engorge ourselves no more at the endlessly refilling buffet. We heaved ourselves back to our suite, grabbed our bags and charged downstairs to reception just in time to load our rucksacks into the waiting taxi.

I heard a voice behind me shout "Mr Ian, Mr Ian,."

I turned, anxiously wondering if there was a late unwelcome addition to our bill.

"Mr Ian, you have forgotten this."

I turned to see a young chambermaid, her hand eagerly extended and face nervously smiling. She was holding Spotty,

Roonagh's favourite toy and our special companion. In our haste, we had left her in our room. This young cheetah was nearly exiled to Hong Kong, never to be seen again. Never mind the loss of the family cat back home, I doubt Roonagh would ever have forgiven us. That chambermaid will never know how grateful we were.

China
Bicycles, balloons and bamboo

A significant amount of research had gone into the best way to enter the People's Republic of China. We knew we were entering the world of Big Brother and bureaucracy.

The hour-long train journey from Hong Kong to the Chinese border proved uneventful, as was our seamless crossing into China through what felt more like a subway station than the access point into the world's largest totalitarian state.

We were heading a few hundred miles deep into rural China and were about to take an internal flight. To reach the airport we had to take what we believed was a short hop in a taxi. According to my research, these would be plentiful. Sure enough, as we emerged from the subway, blinking into the late afternoon Chinese sun, we were met by a cacophony of men eager to direct us to their vehicle.

We settled on one smiling middle-aged man who, in broken English, said, "Follow me Meester."

He led, we followed, rucksacks on our backs and children clinging to our hands. He headed into a multi-storey car park, lightened our load by £60, put our bags in the back of a car and quickly disappeared through a forest of concrete columns. £60 did seem a lot for a short taxi drive, but we had no other option, so we had to take the hit.

I spied our driver in the front seat, a tall, spindly younger man. He beckoned for us to get in the car. Who were we to argue?

The car sped along dual carriageways, bordered by communist bloc concrete blocks in which the people of the People's Republic presumably lived. There was little evidence of human life in the high-rise apartments, but plenty on the roads. We were struck not just by how many cars there were, but how new and modern they appeared.

Twenty minutes in, I started to experience pangs of anxiety and seeds of doubt.

I thought this was supposed to be a short journey. Who is this man? Why wasn't I more assertive back there?

Anne and I couldn't say anything to each other for fear of alarming the kids. I later learnt she was thinking the same thing.

We are being kidnapped by the Chinese Mafia.

As you may well have deduced, we survived. Sure enough, this was no mafia hit. We were not in the clutches of a Triad. It was no more than a lack of sufficient research on my part. Quite simply, the shiny new airport was further away than I had been led to believe. Everything was legit. Thank goodness the kids were oblivious to these shenanigans.

We checked in and proceeded to security, shaken but not stirred. However, this was the day which kept on giving.

Especially for poor Spotty, who we had already nearly abandoned on the other side of the border.

This young cheetah had a beating heart, sewn into her at birth in the *Build a Bear Workshop* back in Edinburgh. Chinese security was clearly unfamiliar with this feature as our hand luggage went through the scanner.

A serious-looking older man, sporting a very officious uniform, moved away from the belt and separated Spotty from the rest of our belongings.

"What is this?" he inquired in broken English. Actually, I lie, he had no command of English, and we had even less Chinese, neither Mandarin nor Cantonese, at our disposal. These were the days before Google Translate. The option to simply whip out our phones and ask him to repeat his request was not available.

Security were concerned about the identity of the internal item they could observe on the X-ray. Could this Western family be drug mules or perhaps be harbouring an explosive device?

At this point, Anne regretted not having done what her mother had. Anne's childhood cuddly toy had a beating heart as well, and her mum had sewn a zip at the back. We feared security was about to disembowel Spotty and give Roonagh further cause to never forgive her parents for the demise of her favourite travelling companion.

Eventually, I channelled my best impression of Marcel Marceau, and successfully conveyed that there was no cause for alarm. Spotty was allowed to proceed unscathed from her latest escapade.

We were the only Westerners on the flight. Which was not the only reason we stood out. Like drinkers in one of those old

Western Movies when a stranger walks through the saloon bar doors, the whole plane stopped as one to gawp open-mouthed at the spectacle before them. We had two children, in a country where the one-child policy was still the law. One child was ginger and the other had long blonde hair. What a freak show.

This reaction was a foretaste of what we would experience throughout China. Everywhere we went, people would stop and stare and often take their cameras out. Sometime surreptitiously. On occasions a queue would form, consisting of locals desperate to have their photo taken with these creatures from another planet. At times I felt like the kids' security detail, controlling the paparazzi swarming around them. "Sorry, form a line please." Then later, "Sorry, last photo, we have to go now."

Landing at a shiny new airport, we were met by a smiling driver holding a board with a variant of my name on it. It was near enough and could only be for us. As we progressed through our travels, we pre-arranged drivers at airports on nearly every occasion. A comfort blanket as we entered each unfamiliar environment.

As we emerged into what should have been darkness, we felt we had, by some trick of time travel, emerged onto the Las Vegas Strip. Luminous electric lights adorned the entire airport terminal in palm trees, panda bears, Christmas trees, the works. Welcome to modern China.

Off our driver sped down a brand-new tarmac road. After ten minutes of smooth driving, the surface mutated into a dirt track until it finally converged with the main highway 30 minutes later. Presumably, the People's Republic had temporarily diverted the road-building budget for the Beijing Olympics. Or they had blown the money on illustrious illuminations.

Although I had allowed insufficient time for us to enjoy the delights of Hong Kong, I overcompensated by booking a nine night stay in the backpacker hot spot of Yangshuo, best known for the stunning limestone *karsts* which dominate the countryside. There are hundreds, if not thousands, of these geological phenomena populating the landscape, punctuated only by rural communities, paddy fields, undulating rivers and rampant over-development.

Once a small fishing village on the banks of the River Li, Yangshuo was now a sprawling conurbation creaking from the impact of mass-tourism, as evidenced by the number of rats we could spot on the stench-ridden riverbanks next to our guesthouse. However, it was a great backpacker destination with loads of shops, cafés, bars, free Wi-Fi and pool tables everywhere and a cool place to hang out for a few days. And a great place to people watch. There were many Chinese tourists, we watched them, and they watched us back.

It transpired that the budget I had diligently researched and constructed all those months ago was way off the mark. Activities were ridiculously expensive, at least when multiplied by four. Reluctantly we restricted ourselves to just two budget blowing activities. The cost-saving decision not to make a side trip to the Dragon Rice Terraces still pains me till this day. Whenever I see photos of those jaw-dropping vistas a pang of regret assaults me.

But we were happy enough chilling out in Yangshuo. We made the most of the cafés and bars, working our way through a diverse range of Chinese and western food. Although not without incident.

Rory has a nut allergy. He had an anaphylactic shock reaction at the age of three when he ate a peanut and always carries an EpiPen. When planning the trip, this worried us. Could we always be guaranteed that the preparation and cooking of his food would be nut-free? We were particularly concerned about Asia. It would be all too easy for nuts to find their way into a curry or sauce. We carried translation cards for countries where we did not have a basic grasp of the language.

It was a week into our time in China before we discovered that the peanut was the principal cooking oil. This critical piece of information had not shown up in my research. Rory suffered no ill effects although we did need to continue to be vigilant and on occasions, ultra-cautious. We had not intended to test the severity of his peanut allergy so far from home, but at least it was not as bad as we had feared.

A few weeks later, sat outside a street café in Bangkok, it was clear our waiter did not understand my request for confirmation that their Thai Green Curry did not contain nuts.

Exasperated, I shouted, "Please tell your Chef that if there are nuts in the food, MY SON WILL DIE."

The curry was nut-free. Or so we believe, Rory pushed it around in the bowl without touching it. To this day, he is not a fan of Thai food, probably psychologically scarred by these events.

Here is a random tip for any traveller, whether backpacking around the world for a year or just going on holiday. Take more than one bank card with you. We had two, one each. Or at least that was the case for half the year. During our week in Yangshuo, one of our two cards was swallowed by an ATM. Despite our best efforts, we could not retrieve it from the bank, perhaps due to our lack of basic Cantonese. Try miming *"My card is stuck in the hole in the wall"* to a bemused Chinese cashier.

Our bank sent a new card to my sister back home. We knew where we would be in a month's time, Bali and arranged for her to send it on. It is fair to say that, while we were waiting for the replacement, every time we used the remaining bank card in an ATM, there was a sense of trepidation. Quite what we would have done if we had lost that card as well is beyond me. The replacement card arrived two days after we left Bali, and we eventually received it in Australia some three months later.

It would be fair to say that our first main activity in Yangshuo was eventful. The day started well and progressed beautifully before nearly ending in complete disaster. We had sourced a local travel guide who met us outside our guest house with four bikes of an acceptable standard. There were no helmets, of course. We were heading for a day in the local countryside just outside Yangshuo. Off we set through the suburban hinterland and were soon in beautiful terrain. Verdant hills and tree-clad limestone karsts pointing to the sky like a forest of Christmas trees.

We boarded two bamboo rafts, a parent and child on each, propelled at a leisurely pace down the karst-fringed river by a young man skilfully steering with a long bamboo pole. We resisted persistent offers to invest in large plastic water pistols from weather-beaten old ladies on the riverside. Unlike the many local tourists who had great fun drenching each other with river water. It was impossible to avoid the complementary headwear, however, conical reed hats. We must have looked comical, but to be fair, they protected us from the blistering heat, although these days sporting them would probably be deemed cultural misappropriation.

After visiting karsts and caves, we cycled back to town. We were no more than five minutes from home when I spotted Rory about to keep going across a junction.

I shouted "Rory, stop, for Christ's sake stop" but he could not hear me over the thundering traffic.

He was blissfully unaware that a large bus was about to turn right, straight into the road he was crossing. Everything stopped and then speeded up to slow-motion. I genuinely thought he was going under the bus. Cold beads of sweat covered my forehead and my mouth felt dry.

It was a blood curdling and spine-chilling moment. The bus did not slow down. Rory did not see it. But fortunately, physics worked in our favour and he safely made it to the other side. We so nearly came close to losing our only son. Of course, he was oblivious to the whole thing.

Passing on a trip to the Dragon Rice Terraces meant we did have enough money for a priority item on our bucket list, a trip in a hot air balloon. A lifetime ambition, something I had always dreamed of.

We nearly missed out as our ride into the great blue yonder was cancelled three times due to low hanging clouds. On our final day in Yangshuo, we were informed that the gods were smiling on us, the stubborn clouds were clearing, and we were good to go.

"At last Daddy, I thought this would never happen. And you promised!"

As we headed beyond the sprawling town into the open countryside, there a sense of excitement in the air.

Suddenly, in the distance, we could see many multi-coloured balloons partially inflated, and then, as we approached the take-off site, an aerial armada drifted over our heads. It was exactly what I had imagined. We couldn't wait.

As we climbed into the wicker basket, I suddenly realised how small it was. The flames ignited, the balloon effortlessly ascended over the karst-studded landscape, and my lifelong vertigo kicked in. The 16 year-old version of me had once frozen rigid at the top of a spiral staircase in the Dome of St Paul's Cathedral in London and literally had to be helped down, completely mortified and totally embarrassed in front of his friends.

Every time any family member held out a hand, or even a finger, past the edge of the basket, I panicked. I felt nauseous, convinced they were about to plunge to certain death, impaled on a karst below.

The rest of the family loved the whole experience. The views of the limestone karsts were breath-taking, the flight of the balloon graceful and the sight of me grimacing hilarious to behold. I will never step into another balloon basket so long as I live. It is funny how sometimes what you dream about does not work out in the way you had imagined.

After what was for the remainder of the family a magical 30 minutes, the balloon started to descend gracefully. We were not the only tourists enjoying this experience. The sky was dotted with three days backlog of punters, like confetti sprinkled over the heads of the lucky couple on their wedding day. I noted the balloon ahead of us looked like it was heading onto the main road. We could spy tiny men furiously stopping traffic like human ants, manically waving their arms and gesturing at cars and trucks to retreat from the impending danger. It quickly transpired that the highway was the impromptu emergency landing site for our balloon. Not quite what we had expected.

When our balloon hit the tarmac, it did so with real force. It lurched onto its side, propelling Anne face first into the gas bottle canister. Whack went her cheek, I honestly thought she had cracked her jawbone or at the very least lost some teeth.

"Oh my God, are you okay?"

She looked at me, eyes bulging, left cheek reddened and the rest of her face pale.

"I think so" she replied. Sure enough, there was no lasting damage other than a beauty of a black eye, but there so nearly could have been. This dramatic landing was the conclusion of our litany of experiences in this beautiful part of rural China.

After another internal flight, we arrived in the heart of Communist China, the capital city, Beijing. We were to experience the city at a unique moment in its history. The 2008 Olympic Games had recently concluded, and the Paralympic Games had just begun.

We had deliberately delayed our visit to Beijing to avoid the Olympics. Prices would be sky high and our tripper budget just would not stand the hit. It had never crossed my mind that by delaying our arrival, our visit would coincide with the Paralympics. This possibility emerged during one of the many chilled bar days in Yangshuo. I quickly flipped back into research mode, and soon found that tickets were available and dirt cheap, targeted at the domestic market.

Timing is everything. We could not have scheduled our visit better. Yes, there were some ethical issues and ones we care about deeply. It was discomforting to stay in the only affordable hotel we could find with a family room. The newly built building was in a block which had recently been Hutongs, traditional small residential alleyways. The government had relentlessly bulldozed them to eliminate hotbeds of dissent and make way for modern developments ahead of the Olympics.

However, from a tripper perspective, we saw Beijing at its best. The Paralympics were in full flow and there was a real buzz about the place. Smog inducing traffic was restricted, rain clouds dispersed with military weaponry, and the city thronged with confused Chinese tourists from the countryside. Bussed in to put bums on seats, they had clearly never seen a big city before, let alone a Western family of four.

We knew in advance that we were likely to attract some attention as a western family with two children. In Yangshuo, a tourist epicentre, it was not too bad. However, I did learn later of another travelling family with four kids, who got so fed up with the constant requests for photos that their children started charging a dollar a snap. Our kids were never so brass-necked but did tire of the entire process. I loved it though, the situation provided fantastic photo opportunities.

From the moment we went to Tiananmen Square on our first evening, the kids were mobbed for photos. It got to the stage where in some places we dare not stand still. Or we would forget, get the kids to pose for a picture for us, and then be stuck for ten minutes as a queue developed of smiling Chinese people all wanting to have their photos taken with them. To this day, there must be photos of our smiling kids adorning mantelpieces right across homes in China.

Moving from Yangshuo to Beijing gave us a fair degree of culture shock.

The authorities had modernised most public toilets especially for the Olympics by installing western sit-down cubicles alongside the existing Asian squats. These new abominations were of no interest to the local women. Anne reported they would form long queues for the squats whilst the sit-downs were unoccupied. Older ladies would leave the door open whilst in full performance. I don't know if this was for security, ventilation or conversational purposes. Perhaps they were chatting with the resident toilet attendant whose purpose was unclear, given the filthy state of every toilet block we entered.

We noticed little kids had a slit in the back of their trousers and did not wear a nappy. We soon realised it was wise to keep our distance, especially on public transport, should nature take its course. The purpose of the slit became clear.

Road safety was a big issue for a travelling family. We quickly established that a green man at a pedestrian crossing signified all traffic turning the corner must proceed at great speed. We learnt that early on. There were bikes everywhere of course, apart from on the expansive Olympic campus where they would have been a great asset. Remarkably we never saw any accidents. An oriental ballet took place in front of our eyes every time we stepped into the street. The performers were pedestrians, bicycles, motorbikes, cars and vans, all weaving between each other in perfect harmony. Once we learned how it all worked, we became bit-part players in this amazing spectacle.

Being vegetarians with a nut-allergic son, we knew it would be challenging to eat well in China. Street stalls serving all manner of animal body parts and insects from cockroaches to scorpions would not be the mainstay of our diet. Wet markets were off-limits, but this was no hardship. The lack of fresh fruit and vegetables surprised us. Because of what we don't eat, we couldn't just wander into a restaurant, point at pictures and take potluck. Most restaurants had laminated pictures of the food outside. It was a lottery identifying what was what in supermarkets. In the end, we found a great pizzeria and ice cream shop in a food court and made repeat visits. No complaints from junior trippers there.

We did the obvious tourist activities in Beijing, and why not, we were tourists after all.

Tiananmen Square, seared in my memory by television images of the 1989 democracy protests and that man in front of that tank. It looked very different now, decked out in full costume for the Games, its vast concrete expanse rammed with excitable domestic tourists.

The Forbidden City, a vast and grand complex in the heart of Beijing just off Tiananmen Square. Memorably portrayed by the grandeur of the 1987 epic movie *The Last Emperor*, directed by Bernardo Bertolucci, about the life of Puyi, the last Emperor of China.

The world's largest temple, the 15th-century Temple of Heaven, set in vast and beautifully tended gardens. It was fun watching the elderly locals enjoying tai chi and playing foot badminton. This sport may have a proper name in China, but it basically involves playing with no net, no rackets, using your feet to propel the shuttlecock to your opponent.

Visiting the Terracotta Warriors had been on our original itinerary but was dropped due to a massive earthquake in Chengdu, capital of the Sichuan province, that fundamentally changed our Asian plans. Finding half a dozen warriors was a surprise bonus, not in Xian several hundred miles from Beijing, but in the Johnson and Johnson sponsored exhibit at the Paralympics.

We had missed almost all of the Olympic Games due to a lack of television access in Madagascar and Mauritius. "Usain who?"

It was time for us to catch up on the summer's sporting events and the Paralympic Games provided us with the perfect opportunity to get up to speed.

On a rainy Tuesday evening, we headed to the futuristic Birds Nest Stadium to see an athletics session and bear witness to the setting of 13 world records. The flood-lit stadium was packed, although it was evident the spectators did not have a clue what was going on. Some of the cheering fans were probably secret police, embedded to encourage the locals to applaud and scream every time a Chinese athlete won. The national anthems were dutifully respected, especially every time the Chinese flag was hoisted in celebration over the winner's podium.

It was awe-inspiring and humbling to watch the Paralympians, each has overcome so much and will have their own story to tell. We loved it so much that we promised the kids we would take them to the next Paralympic Games. We kept that promise in London, four years later.

We returned to the Olympic Park two days later to watch wheelchair basketball. It was the first time the Paralympic Games had ever been hosted in China. We were keen to make the most of the opportunity to experience this unique occasion. Even though our tickets were for 4:00 pm, we were on the Olympic Green by mid-morning. There was a real Chinese festival atmosphere with very few westerners, although there was a massive McDonalds.

The whole of China had come out to play. They posed for photos at every opportunity, making peace signs to the camera as they smiled and preened. Each Chinese province had an exhibition stand where we learnt about culture, costumes and customs. Anne entertained the crowds when she was reluctantly dragged onto the stage to demonstrate her rudimentary skills in Cantonese calligraphy. It was all random and all good.

It was a stiflingly hot day, and by the time the doors opened, we were ready for some respite in the air-conditioned National Indoor Stadium. We enjoyed two matches. Firstly, Canada versus Iran and then the hosts against Brazil. The atmosphere was fantastic, the chant *Let's Go China* sounded to us like *China, Jungle Dave,* and we embarrassed the kids by joining in. As the only western family in the arena, we appeared on the giant screen several times, so were probably famous right around China as our faces were beamed into every home around the country.

Wheelchair basketball is fantastic, fierce and fun. The players charge into each other like rampaging rhinos, frequently knocking their competitors to the ground. It was like watching a game of human dodgems. Sometimes it was hard not to look away as collisions led to the players flying through the air and crashing to the ground. The sound of crunching metal smashing into the hard concrete floor reverberated around the arena. But these warriors hardly blinked, they just flicked themselves upright and got back to work.

During an interval, I bumped, not literally, into the Australian comedian, Adam Hills. We had something in common, as he was a regular performer at the Edinburgh Fringe Festival, and I had seen him there many times. He was commentating on the games for Australian television. We chatted for a good 20 minutes and he told me that wheelchair basketball was his new favourite sport. It was hard not to agree. It was fast, furious and fair.

We left Beijing's best attraction of all till last. The Great Wall of China is so big that you can see it from outer space, so we didn't go to all of it. We headed to a stretch of the wall called Mutianyu, arriving shortly after sunrise, with hardly any other tourists to bother us. We walked and climbed for three hours in bright sunshine in the most stunning of landscapes. Neither words nor pictures cannot do this place justice, it was simply breath-taking.

The only downer was that the previous evening, Anne had misplaced her footing on a step on the way out of the Olympic Park, taken a tumble and damaged her knee. As a result, she hobbled up and down the Great Wall in significant pain, becoming our very own Terracotta Warrior.

This was no mean feat. The wall was not a flat and smooth surface and it undulated like a rollercoaster. There were hundreds of steps along the way to make things worse for her. These steps were not the same height, that would have made things too easy. Some were tiny and others huge, it was random and must have induced even more pain for her. Although we arrived early, the sun soon started to heat up, which couldn't have helped walking conditions.

We learnt that pain can be overcome when the prize is great enough, even if only for a little while.

There was a reward. Anne didn't have to walk down. We all had the unique experience of tobogganing down the Great Wall of China. Now that's not something you do every day. What an amazing way to end our time in China, holding on for dear life, screaming and laughing as we sped around the bends ready for the next stage of our adventures.

Japan
The wrong castle

We adored Japan. Very much. It was Anne's favourite country of the entire year. Quirky, clean and polite. That is an excellent description of my lovely wife. And of Japan. Highly regulated, connected and advanced. That is Japan, not Anne.

Japan has a glorious and troubled history, the latter of which it appears to have put firmly in the past. A fascinating mix of ancient and modern, of East meets West. America meets Japan in a quintessentially Japanese way. John and Yoko on steroids, figuratively speaking.

Basing ourselves in Tokyo, we made a significant investment in a family rail pass for our two weeks in Japan. We divided our time between working our way through the city's most interesting districts and visiting locations further afield. To be honest, we never stopped. Japan was the gift that just kept on giving, and in a fortnight, we only scratched the surface.

We felt more at home here than in China. People gazed at us curiously but not censoriously as we walked along with our two offspring. Anne, a petite and perfectly formed five-foot high woman, was taller than many of the local ladies. Six inches higher, I felt like I was average height for once in my life.

The cost of living is notoriously high, especially in Tokyo. To give you a flavour, a fruity flavour, of the cost of living, one melon would have set us back £50 in a department store food hall. To be fair, the price did include gift wrapping. Historically, fruit played a significant role in the nation's gift-giving culture. During the 14th century, samurais would offer tangerines or melons to the shogun, their leader, as a sign of loyalty and appreciation.

We would visit the food hall when we were peckish, it had a fantastic range of free tastings. What's not to like when living on a backpacker budget.

Our living space for the fortnight was microscopic, the tiniest apartment in which we have ever stayed. We are all diminutive in stature, yet it was still necessary to walk sideways into the bathroom, and the galley kitchen was so narrow there was only space for one person at a time. And no swinging cats. It was a good job we were still getting on with each other.

The 2008 global financial crisis was raging. I started to question my reckless decision to quit a secure and well-paid job to become an unpaid itinerant traveller. We had one pot of money and our bank balance was only heading in one direction. Suddenly my prospects of picking up a good position when we got home were looking dicey and I had a wobble. I started looking for vacancies back home and even applied for one. We could end the trip early, or Anne could continue with the kids, and I would go back home and provide an income whilst there were still roles available.

It felt like the world was about to end and we were heading back into The Great Depression of the 1930s. Our return home would be like stepping into the pages of a Steinbeck novel unless I could get this job. The agency handling the vacancy refused to interview me via video call, as primitive as this might now sound. This rejection proved to be a blessing in disguise, and we kept going. It was a great decision, even though I was unemployed for a year on our return home.

The kids found the international news fascinating. We had Cable TV in our capsule of an apartment, and they became hooked, not just on *The Simpsons*, but also CNN. Their first question each morning would be "Has the bailout bill been passed by Congress yet?" or "Who won the debate last night, Obama or McCain?" If there were any lingering doubts that they would get a great education from life on the road, this episode put those worries to bed.

Anyway, back to our travels. Japan was bountiful in its propensity to stimulate our senses and bring smiles to our faces. Quite simply, it was like nowhere else we had visited.

No place was more unique than the historic and spiritual city of Kyoto, the Japan of Shogun, Samurai and Geishas. The Japan of our dreams. There are more temples per square kilometre here than anywhere else on earth. We only had time to visit five out of the seventeen. Lightweights, I know.

We loved these Zen temples. They were tranquil, historic and well, zen-like. We visited the historic Gion district at dusk, wandering along streets where the 2005 movie *Memoirs of a Geisha* was filmed. Traditionally dressed Geisha girls hurried past in the twilight. These young ladies, intricately dressed and highly made-up, appeared so shy as they gracefully sped past, yet were professional entertainers trained in traditional styles of Japanese performing art. Their distinctive appearance comprised a colourful kimono, classic hairstyles and theatrical make-up. Not tourist attractions, nor prostitutes as is commonly perceived in the West, but a kaleidoscopic glimpse into Japan's imperial past.

Less successful was a day trip to Mount Fuji, Japan's iconic mountain that features on so many images of the country. We purchased an all-inclusive ticket combining all available modes of transport to complete a loop circuit of the mountain. It ended up feeling like just another travel day for the Family Trippers, and due to low clouds, we never saw the legendary mountain.

For the record, we travelled on two bullet trains, three local trains, one funicular, one bus, three cable cars and a pirate ship across a volcanic lake. Apart from the pirate ship, the day's highlight was eating blackened eggs cooked in a volcanic pool. The kids were not sure which was worse, the smell of the eggs, the stench of sulphur in the air or Anne's repulsed face.

After extensive online research, we also went to the nearby city of Yokohama to watch a J League football match at the venue for the 2002 World Cup Final. As we walked from the train station, it felt eerily quiet. We thought it a little odd when, 90 minutes before kick-off, no fans were milling around the stadium, no one proudly wearing scarves or replica shirts. I knew J League matches did not draw huge crowds, but even so, something was not right. There was nobody to ask where everybody was, so we wandered around for a while before giving in and heading back to Tokyo. It turns out Yokohama have two grounds and play their home matches alternately at each. And this Saturday was the turn of the other stadium. We were in the wrong place.

Aside from day trips using our rail pass, the novelty of living in the quirky and stimulating metropolis of Tokyo kept us busy. We dragged the regularly reluctant kids around museums, galleries and skyscrapers, shopping malls, ancient temples and high-tech electrical shops galore. Everything was different from back home, fresh, exciting and stimulating. We experienced sensory overload and loved it.

There was, however, one defining moment which occurred on an excursion away from the capital city.

Three months in, and this was the moment I had been putting off. Like a constipated ostrich, head in the sand and buttocks clenched. We were on the bullet train, making the most of our rail pass. I decided it would be a good idea to review our budget. A growing necessity because Rory, who kept a daily tally of our spends as part of his mental maths challenge, would sometimes deny me an evening beer by gleefully declaring we had already exhausted that day's allowance. Boy, would I soon need a beer.

I pulled out our trusty companion, the battered and bruised laptop. Firing her up, I loaded that spreadsheet. The one I had been avoiding, insanely blinded by vain denial. Suddenly my heart almost stopped. My brow moistened. Constipation was suddenly no longer a problem. I realised I had made a monumental error six months earlier when I set our budget.

I had swapped a month in China for a month in Australia, the latter being a more expensive destination. I had not accounted for this when the Chengdu earthquake struck and we had to shorten our scheduled stay in China, including missing out on seeing Giant Pandas, which had been the catalyst for China's inclusion in our itinerary in the first place.

In an instant, I could see what I had done wrong but never spotted. Our contingency budget was wiped out. We had already spent it and our planned dream trips to the Galápagos Islands, to Angkor Wat in Cambodia and several other magical places had vanished in a flash. We did not have the funds and would not be able to go.

I sheepishly looked at Anne and nervously said, "You won't believe what I've gone and done?"

It is a good job I have a forgiving wife. She just shrugged her shoulders and replied, "What's the worst that can happen?"

The highlight of our time in Japan was an overnight trip to the historic and tragic city of Hiroshima.

Let's get out the way the slight inconvenience we endured on arrival. The two sweltering nights we spent in a stiflingly stuffy hotel room that barely had space for four mattresses on the floor, with the air conditioning temperature dial stuck on 28 degrees centigrade. Despite this sleep deprivation, we awoke recharged if not refreshed from restless troubled dreams, and Hiroshima took our breath away.

Hiroshima is notorious for the event which occurred at 8:15 am on 6th August 1945. The American Bomber, *Enola Gay,* dropped the world's first deployed atomic bomb directly overhead and obliterated the city in a heartbeat. 80,000 citizens below perished instantaneously. Before the year was out, 200,000 people were dead. Tens of thousands more would die from the effects of radiation, or experience life-limiting illnesses in the years ahead.

President Barack Obama, on his visit to Hiroshima, delivered a passionate speech opening with these evocative words:

"Seventy-one years ago, on a bright cloudless morning, death fell from the sky and the world was changed. A flash of light and a wall of fire destroyed a city and demonstrated that mankind possessed the means to destroy itself."

Along with Nagasaki, which suffered the same fate three days later, Hiroshima serves as the best possible deterrent against nuclear weapons. We were all shocked to learn that in the 1980s the Soviet Union tested a single bomb which was 17 times more powerful than all those used in World War II and 3,100 times more powerful than the bomb that exploded over Hiroshima.

On his visit to Hiroshima in 1981, the late Pope John Paul II wrote:

War is the work of man
War is destruction of human life
War is death
To remember the past is to commit oneself to the future
To remember Hiroshima is to abhor nuclear war
To remember Hiroshima is to commit oneself to peace

When the bomb exploded 600 metres above Hiroshima on that bright summer's morning, everything and everyone in its direct path perished under the 5,000-degree heat. Incredibly the frame of one building, the *A Bomb Dome*, survives to this day, its charred shell serving as a poignant memorial to the horrors of that fateful morn.

We spent an emotional yet informative visit in the Peace Park and Museum, an experience which will stay with us all for the rest of our lives. Sitting in a vast chapel reading the names of some of the victims, standing in front of a large clock, its hands stopped at 15 minutes past eight, were chilling moments and tears flowed. Parts of the museum were just too upsetting, and I took the kids away while Anne, a member of the Campaign for Nuclear Disarmament in her student days, lingered to learn more and weep buckets.

The following morning, we took a boat trip across Hiroshima Bay to Miyajima Island. Featured heavily in the 1967 Bond film *You Only Live Twice*, the island is famous for its bright red Zen Arch which dramatically emerges from the waves lapping at its feet. There were wild deer everywhere, peppered around the colourful temples and wooded hillsides. Rory was fascinated by these friendly creatures and was soon missing in action with the family camera, taking some amazing close-up shots.

On the return journey to Tokyo, we stopped off at Himeji Castle. This classic 17th-century Japanese castle is unusual because, unlike most old Japanese buildings bombed during the war, it is still the original. Sean Connery got here before us, as it also featured in the Bond movie.

Roonagh had been looking forward to visiting Himeji for nine months. Her class had been doing a project on castles and she had seen this one in a book. "We are going to Japan, Roonagh. I will make sure we go there" I promised her as we had read together one evening.

As we walked out of the train station and peered down the long road towards the castle, I proudly boasted, "See, I promised you, didn't Daddy do well."

Her response stopped me in my tracks, "That's the wrong castle Daddy."

Indeed it was, I had brought her all this way and then ended up at a different castle from the one she had been so looking forward to.

We had swerved visiting Giant Pandas at Hong Kong Zoo because we could see them in Beijing. But the Paralympics got in the way and we ran out of time. We reassured the kids we could still see them in Tokyo. This was a big deal for them. Pandas being the original reason China had made the itinerary. They were on that list they gave us in that Turkish bar. But then the Chengdu earthquake happened, meaning we couldn't visit the Giant Panda Research Centre and see cute baby cubs with their parents.

As we arrived at Ueno Zoo gates, I spotted a chalkboard sign with English writing on it. Maybe it was important information? It was.

We are sorry to announce that our Panda Bear died in April.

I was probably more devastated than the kids. I felt entirely responsible, not for this panda's unfortunate demise, which patently wasn't my fault. But just for letting them down again. They were stoical and quickly bounced back after a few initial tears. We all put a brave face on it, had a great day at the zoo, and made do with the cute red pandas instead. But they were a poor substitute.

A few days later, after yet more research, we took a 3.5 hour train journey to Kobe to another smaller zoo where the odyssey could finally end, and we did see a pair of Pandas. It was a relief to be able to tick this item off our bucket list.

As soon as we arrived at the zoo, we were concerned about animal welfare, given the distressed state of the big cats pacing up and down. The pandas themselves looked exactly as they do on TV, but rather than being in a natural setting, as they would have been in China, they were behind reflective glass in a large concrete box. They were asleep and facing the wrong direction. It was a disappointing experience.

The lesson here is to keep us away from these unique animals. We are bad news. A couple of years later, I learnt these Pandas had died, following an artificial insemination procedure which went tragically wrong. It wasn't a massive surprise.

The irony was that shortly after our return home to Scotland, Edinburgh Zoo housed two Giant Pandas on a ten year lease from the Chinese Government. Our panda hunt around the world ended up being entirely unnecessary.

We learnt a great deal about Japanese culture in our two weeks, although I suspect we only scratched the surface of this highly sophisticated and at times mysterious society. Especially mysterious for overseas visitors on a short break. There is an intricate and often impenetrable etiquette that is important to comprehend as a culturally sensitive visitor.

We learnt it is rude to sneeze or blow your nose in public, strong character being the hallmark of a man who can keep it in. Sniffing, however, is encouraged.

It is rude to eat in public, other than in restaurants. We were met with sneering disapproval when we ate our lunchtime butties perched on a wall by a park, this by a woman who was wiping her dog's backside with a tissue.

Eating on a train, on the other hand, is permitted. You should open your briefcase, take out a tablecloth, dress the table as if in a restaurant, before tucking into your bento box.

Bowing is a sign of deference. When the immaculately uniformed ticket conductor enters your train carriage, expect a deep bow and a short incantation. A taxi driver dressed more like a chauffeur will end your journey with the same polite gesture. The deeper the bow, the greater the respect. He, for it will be a he, will be sartorially elegant in perfectly pressed trousers, peaked cap perched on his well-coiffured head with hands ensconced in immaculately clean white gloves.

After two inspiring and informative weeks, the Rising Sun set on our Japanese adventure. We departed Japan for what we hoped will not be the final time as we headed off for some welcome rest and relaxation in the Indonesian island of Bali before hitting the orangutan trail in Borneo.

Bali
Read your emails

Transferring to Bali from Tokyo was not as smooth as we had hoped. I lived in constant fear of mixing up one of our bookings. Only a few days earlier I had joked to Anne, "This planning lark is going too well, I just hope I don't go and cock it up." I wish I'd kept my mouth shut.

Following an eight hour flight to Kuala Lumpur for an overnight stopover before our flight to Bali, we arrived at the five-star Pan Pacific Hotel's check-in desk at 9:00 pm. Our flight the next day was at 11:30 am so I figured it made sense to spend the night in an airport hotel. I was so proud I had found one where you checked in at the baggage hall.

That pride was short-lived.

"Mr Pilbeam? No, we have no reservation in that name Sir."

It transpired I had instead booked the Grand Pacific Hotel downtown, an hour's taxi ride away in central Kuala Lumpur. I had a dawning realisation that my time had come, and I had made a mess of a booking.

Because of my mix-up, we had to scrap the Grand Pacific, sacrifice our deposit and pay a small ransom to stay at the Pan Pacific instead. No family rooms were available, so we were given a triple and Rory slept in an armchair.

The next morning, I woke early. The kids were fast asleep, and Anne was in the shower. She wanted to maximise the value of the luxury bathroom and pamper herself. I popped on the television in our room to check the departure board. Our flight was nowhere to be seen. Slightly concerned, I popped down to reception to ask the concierge - yes, the hotel was that posh - what time our flight would be leaving. He smirked and said, "Sir, this is the main International Terminal. You need the Low-Cost Terminal, which is a 20-minute taxi ride away." Based on his demeanour and well-rehearsed response, it was obviously not the first time he had been posed this question by an imbecilic traveller.

I checked my watch, the time was 9:45 am and there were less than two hours until flight time.

"Right, stay calm, it will all be fine. We can make it," I thought as I charged across the hotel lobby, into the first available lift and down the hallway to our room. Or maybe I just panicked.

I burst into our room, dragged the kids out of bed and shouted to Anne, "Don't ask any questions, don't argue, just get your clothes, we have to leave NOW."

Anne was halfway through shaving her legs, with one leg still fully lathered. Five minutes later, bed hair intact and teeth unbrushed, off we all sped in the first available taxi to the Low-Cost Terminal.

We made it to the check-in desk with two minutes to spare. Relieved, we proceeded directly to security.

Only then did I remember I had treated myself to a large bottle of single malt at Tokyo airport. Because it was duty-free, I still had it in my hand luggage. Tell a lie, it was in Rory's hand luggage. I faced the choice of ditching the whisky or checking in Rory's bag. There was no way I was losing that bottle of Glenlivet, my tipple of choice, so I charged back to the check-in desk and sweet-talked the attendant into checking-in Rory's bag.

I then panicked for the entire flight as I realised that, alongside the precious glass bottle, were the kids' diaries of our first three months' travels. What would happen if the bottle smashed in transit and the kids' special memories were destroyed forever? I would never have forgiven myself.

On arrival at Denpasar Airport, I nervously paced up and down as we waited by the luggage carousel for our bags to arrive. As always seemed to be the case, ours were last to appear. Would the whisky bottle be intact, or would we discover a worrying dark stain on the outside of Rory's bag? All was well, the bottle was not broken, and at least one thing had gone to plan that day.

It may be a popular holiday destination for Australians, but the tropical island of Bali is much more than that. It is the only non-Muslim of the 13,000 islands comprising the Indonesian archipelago, attracting a quarter of all tourists visiting Indonesia. The fusion of tourism, complex history and a unique adaptation of Hinduism, render this a fascinating destination. We planned to come to Bali for nine nights, but another of my administrative errors led to an extended stay. More on that later.

As was now our habit, I had organised a taxi that was dutifully waiting for us at the airport and transported us through the built-up southern end of the island into Bali's cultural heartland and the small touristy town of Ubud.

Our hotel was in a paddy field on the outskirts of town and looked like a historical monument. It turned out *Nick's Hidden Cottages* was the same age as Roonagh. A closer look revealed the tell-tale sign of breeze blocks behind the ornate facades. Misshapen mattresses were scattered across the dusty concrete floor, delightfully accompanied by the pitter-pattering feet of curious cockroaches.

Ubud was reminiscent of Yangshuo in China, with a saturation of tourist facilities, frequent power cuts, and the all too frequent whiff of an over-worked sewage system. We felt guilty about being part of the problem.

One morning, whilst out on an explore around the outskirts of town, we came across a traditional Balinese cremation ceremony, set in Ubud's Monkey Forest. It was a huge, colourful event that assaulted all of our senses. A significant occasion in Balinese culture treated by the local population as a celebratory affair.

Hundreds of locals participated in the intricate rituals unperturbed by camera-wielding tourists, the loud voices of tour guides corralling their paying punters and even a squealing piglet skewered to a stick. The ceremony had many chapters, curated to ensure the soul of the departed embarked on its journey to the afterworld, accompanied by a plethora of worldly gifts such as flowers, aromatic scent and trinkets. It was an enthralling experience, setting all my senses on fire, figuratively not literally. The sounds, the smells, the sights were like nothing I had ever experienced. My touch was unaffected though- I kept a respectful distance from the mourners.

The culmination of the proceedings was the lighting of the funeral pyre with large flame torches. It was all too much for the younger trippers. They headed to a nearby café for a round of cokes with their Mum, leaving me to brandish my camera as considerately as possible in such revered surroundings. Less reverential were the forest's inhabitants. Like a plague of locusts, the monkeys swarmed everywhere, availing themselves of all edible sacraments.

Having double checked my guidebook, it turned out that the Sacred Monkey Forest was one of the must-see sights in Bali. We returned the following morning to visit the boisterous inhabitants. Lively little fellows, they would rob you of a banana as much as look at you. There were signs everywhere warning visitors not to feed them. We complied, unlike some other tourists who soon found themselves assaulted by the eager residents. It reminded the kids of the monkey soldier scene in *The Wizard of Oz*. These primates could sure get a move on, even without wings.

Tourist towns like Ubud do what they say on the tin, with attractions like the traditional *legong* and *barong* dancing show, a colourful affair. We arrived early to bag the best vantage position in the majestic outdoor Royal Palace, only for a torrential downpour meaning the event had to be relocated to a local school gymnasium just before curtains-up. The show was impressive and young Roonagh, a keen ballet dancer, was especially enthralled. The costumes were elaborate, the movements graceful, the story relatively easy to follow. And we did our best not to be distracted by the sizeable live hog, carried just to the left of our seats whilst tethered to a bamboo pole, fiercely and noisily protesting at its imminent and inevitable fate.

After four nights in Ubud, we took a southbound taxi-transfer to the family beach resort of Sanur for a relaxed stay in an Australian owned hotel.

Asia was a treasure trove of well-practised street-sellers who were evidently vastly experienced in entertainingly engaging foreign visitors with rhetorical refrains such as "where do you come from?," "are you from Germany?" along with other classics such as "lovely jubbly" and "looky Asda price."

Occasionally we would concede we were from Scotland, only to be told our new best friend had a cousin with a restaurant in Glasgow, although they could never tell us exactly where. If we said we were from the UK, this was often heard as The Ukraine. Occasionally, just for fun, we would invent our country of origin and claim we were from Australia, Belgium or Sweden.

We still joke today at the audacity of one overzealous stallholder who remarked Anne was a dead ringer for Hillary Clinton. Sorry Bill, but Mama Tripper did not take being called your wife's doppelganger as a compliment.

We took full advantage of the bonus days we ended up having in Bali due to the flight reschedule and mainly lounged about in the tropical sun. Being a proud Balinese and keen to earn a bit of money on the side, the hotel manager was eager to show us the island. He took us on a day trip to the north where we visited a Royal Palace, a waterfall with the unfortunate name *Git Git* and some so-called *holy* thermal baths. I say '*so-called*' because they were only a couple of steps up in cleanliness from Madagascar's communal bathtub.

Bali was in danger of being spoiled by over-tourism. In the south of the island, this had already happened to some extent. It faced the classic dilemma in a globalised world where travel is cheap and accessible, and the tourist dollar is needed for the island to be economically sustainable. Much of the island was, however, relatively unspoilt.

It was heartening to see how deep-rooted the Balinese version of Hinduism was, a series of spiritual beliefs and rituals at the very heart of Balinese daily life.

Every home had a temple, sometimes several. Each village had three large temples. Palm baskets, regularly replenished with exotic flowers and fruit, adorned every doorstep and street corner. Incense filled the air and there were constant religious celebrations everywhere.

Alcohol tax was punitive in this Muslim country. A bottle of Jacobs Creek wine was triple the cost of Australia and even double the price of Japan. Fortunately, alcohol did not have a massive impact on our budget. This was a family trip after all, not a year of expensive cocktails. Remember Rory held the purse strings. The kids were more interested in ice-cream, cold drinks and pizza.

Rory had one unfortunate incident in Japan which required attention in Bali. He had bitten into an olive bread roll near the end of our time in Japan and cracked a tooth on an olive stone. We knew it would be prohibitively expensive to get emergency dental care in Japan, so we put it off until Bali. We imagined having to communicate with a traditional doctor in a hut in some remote village. However, the south of the island was very tourist-friendly, and after a brief visit to a sparkling clean dental clinic, he left with a repaired tooth and his parents just £10 lighter.

Our original plan had been to spend nine days in Bali, before a two week trip to the neighbouring island of Borneo. And that would have happened if I had read my emails correctly.

Lesson: when your airline sends an email entitled "*Urgent*", READ IT! It might not be marketing spam or just a flight confirmation.

It might be an itinerary change.

Or even a cancellation.

We learnt that harsh lesson not once, but twice.

One afternoon I dragged myself away from our hotel pool because it was time to check-in for our Air Asia flight to Borneo the next day. *That's strange,* I thought. I couldn't find the flight on their website.

Oh no, here we go again.

I checked and checked again. No, it wasn't there. I phoned the Air Asia customer helpline. It transpired the airline had withdrawn that route two months previously and there was no flight at all. Sure enough, on checking my deleted folder, there was the email confirming the route cancellation.

I did a quick google and established that flying to Indonesian Borneo would now cost £1,500. We talked it through, changed our plan and stayed another week in Bali. The new plan was to head to Kuala Lumpur in Malaysia for a few days before a truncated experience in Malaysian Borneo. Although it was frustrating to write off a wildlife extravaganza I had planned and paid for, we were comforted by the knowledge that we would still have the opportunity to experience Borneo's delights.

I would love to say that we left Bali refreshed and rejuvenated. That would have been the case if it were not for a rather unpleasant tropical bug that made Anne and the kids violently ill and would later infect me in Borneo.

My lasting recollection of checking-in at Denpasar Airport for our rearranged flight to Kuala Lumpur was whispering to Anne, perched on her haunches with a pale white face and watery eyes, "Stand up, stand up. They won't let you on the flight."

On arrival at our hotel in the Malaysian capital, Anne went straight to bed for three days.

Malaysia
Kuala Lumpur's delights

Kuala Lumpur, a weekend in the Malaysian capital, sandwiched between more exotic trips to Bali and Borneo. A stopover destination for many Asian travellers, even though the airport is 74 kilometres from the city.

With Anne confined to her sickbed, Roonagh joined her when the first assault of smog-heavy humidity knocked her for six. The boys hit the town. Rory had been the first to be felled by whatever bug this was and was therefore ahead of the curve with his recovery. I was seemingly immune.

We stayed in a poky family room overlooking a bustling street market in the city's vibrant, raucous and bouncing Chinatown. Even though we had been to China, this was our first real authentic Chinese street market experience. It proved an excellent location for another futile search for great vegetarian Chinese food and to shop for a wide range of knock off gear. Branded football shirts, bags and jewellery were plentiful amongst the unethical yet budget-friendly options.

Our overall impression of Kuala Lumpur was a juxtaposition of oil-derived wealth and crushing poverty. The transport infrastructure was first class, and we made great use of the modern Skyline Tram system, similar to the type connecting terminals at large international airports. Yet looking down on the smelly Klang River, we saw all sorts of detritus flowing along, including on one occasion a fridge and a double mattress. It is perhaps no coincidence that Kuala Lumpur is Malay for *muddy confluence*.

Three notable landmarks dominated the city's surprisingly low-rise skyline. We could see the KL Tower, the world's fourth largest communications tower, from our hotel bedroom window. Then there were the iconic Petronas Towers, the tallest twin towers in the world, connected by a glass sky bridge, itself the world's highest double storey bridge. Add to this an array of spectacular onion-domed mosques, their minarets serving as signposts around the city landscape. As with any great city, the cityscape looked impressive by day and stunning when illuminated at night.

The impressive 88 storeys high Petronas Towers, glass shining like a diamond tiara glinting in the glare of paparazzi flashbulbs at the Oscars, are a permanent reminder that oil is a vital part of the economy of this major Asian city. We did manage to get Anne and Roonagh well enough, after a couple of days recuperation, to visit these iconic towers.

While waiting for our time slot to ride the *Charlie and the Chocolate Factory* style glass elevator up the Petronas Towers, Anne had an opportunity to get a much-desired haircut. Her carefully styled bob is her signature piece, a crucial part of her identity, and she is often stopped by women enquiring where she gets it cut. A salon in the shopping malls of the Petronas Towers was to provide her best answer yet. She stumbled upon the only ex-London salon artistic director in Malaysia who had a late cancellation. It turned out this guy cut celebrities' hair, including ex-British Prime Minister Tony Blair and the Spice Girls. Anne got her hair cut by Victoria Beckham's hairdresser. For £20. How cool is that.

KL, as it is commonly known, provided a reminder of one of the many reasons I am so reliant on Anne to keep me right. When Anne and Roonagh had recovered, we were keen to experience local cuisine. The first place we walked into in Chinatown looked great to me, but Anne took one look at the dirty, sticky tables and the chaos in the kitchen at the rear, and declared, "We're leaving. Now."

My next top pick was a cute street café with outside tables near the edge of a vibrant night food market. It was not cute in my eagle-eyed wife's view though, spying the dishes being washed outside in dirty water. I was told to keep moving. Given the illness she was just recovering from, she was right to be cautious. What a good job she had not born witness to some of the establishments I had dined in during my time in Sri Lanka earlier that year and to think I was only hospitalised once with a stomach upset.

As we boarded the short internal flight to Kota Kinabalu in Malaysian Borneo, with two healthy kids alongside us and Anne neatly coiffured and recuperated, I felt a sense of excitement at the adventures ahead in the land of orangutans. I also felt a strange gurgling in my lower stomach.

Borneo
Uno, Uno, Uno

Sometimes you can build somewhere up so much in your imagination it can't live up to your expectations. Well, that was Borneo, at least for us. Maybe me being horribly ill didn't help. Perhaps if we had another couple of grand to do all the exciting, but ridiculously expensive, eco-activities it would have been brilliant.

The bug belatedly floored me as we arrived in Kota Kinabulu, one of the places I had been most looking forward to visiting. This nature-based bonanza was going to be amazing. Sadly, it didn't work out that way. I still don't feel I have been to Borneo and it remains unfinished business.

I had pictured Rory and I doing an overnight ascent of the magnificent 4,000 metres high Kinabulu mountain which sits magnificently over rainforest a few miles away from the sprawling town. We would stay in the overnight lodge on its slopes, then wake at 3:00 am to ascend by torchlight to reach the summit in time for a life-affirming sunrise over the tropical jungle below, cementing our male bond as intrepid explorers sharing this once in a lifetime experience together. Father and son at the top of the world.

In reality, my legs were so weak I could hardly climb the stairs from the scruffy reception desk to the first floor of the shabby Hotel London, which was not as grand as its name. After 24 hours of me sitting on the floor alongside the leaking toilet cistern, accompanied by cockroaches scuttling across the cracked bathroom tiles, we checked out and moved down the road to the luxury Sabah Hotel. A rare reunion with carpets and large comfy beds and just what the doctor ordered. Every morning I ventured downstairs to the buffet breakfast, shuffling a barely nibbled slice of toast around my plate before returning to my comfy bed. But each day got better, and with time, I recovered.

These were no doubt long days for Anne, entertaining two kids with little to do. But she also recalls they were fun times, hanging out, playing countless rounds of Uno and mucking around in the hotel pool. However, one such swimming session was prematurely ended by the arrival of a local caiman. For those unfamiliar with caiman, they are basically a smaller relative of crocodiles and alligators. Not the sort of swimming buddy I would wish for my kids. Or anybody's kids.

We were also all Asia'd out. I love Asia, it is exciting, stimulating and provides sensory overload. But for us northern Europeans perhaps there is only so much hustle, heat and humidity we can take before we need a rest. We were nearly three months in, I had spent six months of the year in Asia, and we were ready to get back to the West for a bit. The opportunity to stop for a few days and reflect led to us changing our plans. After a month in Thailand and Singapore, bypassing Vietnam altogether due to our concerns about Rory's nut allergy, we would head to Australia two months early for an extended three month stay.

Anyway, back to Borneo. Malaysian Borneo to be precise.

The island of Borneo is the third-largest island in the world, which you will know by now if you did your research earlier when reading that Madagascar is the fourth largest.

The Borneo landmass is home to three nations.

The oil-rich kingdom state of Brunei occupying just 1% of the island.

Indonesian Borneo, comprising the vast majority of the territory, 73% in total.

To the north, Malaysian Borneo where Kota Kinabulu and the Family Trippers could be found.

We had planned to visit both Borneos, but the flight kerfuffle meant we were restricted to a one-week Malaysian experience.

Kota Kinabulu was a fascinating place close to lush rainforests, tropical islands and the eponymous mountain. And a Starbucks which had free Wi-Fi and provided an alternative homeschool location for Anne and the kids when the mini alligator monster decided it fancied a dip. Maybe they swapped playing Uno for a game of Snap. Yes, that is a bad Dad Joke. No wonder they were glad to spend time with their Mum.

The bay was full of stilt villages, housing just a small number of the city's half a million inhabitants including fishermen who brought home the daily catch of exotic sea creatures. A smoky barbecued aroma permeated the air around the colourful markets lining the shore in the evening, as the most dramatic of orange and red-hued sunsets dominated the South China Sea skyline.

On the outskirts of town, the modern road was lined with slums comprising hundreds of scrap metal shacks that did not appear strong enough to withstand even the slightest of breezes, let alone the monsoons frequenting these shores. These inadequate dwellings were home to migrants from troubled Asian regions and were another painful reminder of how fortunate we were.

What about the orangutans? I am pleased to say we did meet one of the world's smartest primates. Did you know orangutans craft umbrellas out of leaves when it is about to rain?

We visited a local rehabilitation centre at feeding time. The kids were excited when a dozen or so animals swung through the jungle trees in search of their lunch of bananas and tropical fruit. The experience felt natural and well managed, as close as feasible to visiting these splendid yet seriously endangered creatures in the wild.

One orange couple performed their part in ensuring the survival of the species. No need to avert the kids' eyes, this was another example of homeschooling on the road, this time Biology class. It was steamy, but that was because of the intense humidity.

Next time, for I hope there will be a next time, we will do Borneo properly. With a holiday budget, we will take a boat into the jungle to see the orangutans swing across the waterways, hear the unique birdlife and visit the comically long-nosed proboscis monkeys.

My blog for Borneo concluded with *Err, and that's it! Sorry to not have more to tell. We know we're still pretty darn lucky though- we could be at home in the economic and winter gloom after all. And we have seen some amazing tropical downpours from the rather posh Sabah Hotel.*

Cambodia
And the plan changed

Where were you when you heard the historic news that Barack Obama had been elected as the USA's first African American President?

It's one of those classic questions, like *"where were you when you heard JFK had been shot?"*

Answer: not born yet in my case.

"Where were you when man landed on the moon?"

Answer: in my cot.

"Where were you when John Lennon was murdered?"

Answer: in bed, to be woken to the news by my mother.

"Where were you when you heard the Twin Towers had been attacked on 9/11?"

Answer: in an airport lounge about to board the last flight allowed in UK airspace on that fateful day.

Our kids will always be able to give the rather cool answer that the day President Obama was elected, they were crossing the border between Thailand and Cambodia. We watched his victory speech on a small black and white television set whilst our passports were stamped. Everybody cheered when the news broke. One German traveller said to me in a Bangkok café that evening, "it's a good day for the world."

Wait, just a minute. We couldn't afford to go to Angkor Wat in northern Cambodia. That was one of the casualties of my budgeting calamity. Or was it?

One hot sticky afternoon, while visiting the vast temple complex within Bangkok's Imperial Grand Palace, we looked mournfully at a replica model of the Angkor Wat complex. I wistfully said to Anne, "Sorry honey, we were supposed to be going there, and now we never will, and it's all my fault."

Returning to our hotel, I noticed the excursions desk had a sign for trips to Angkor Wat. Ten hours each way by road, visa, three nights hotel, and a tour of the temples for £100 per person. Little thought was needed. I calculated the cost of spending the same amount of time in Bangkok and bingo, we were going to Angkor Wat for free. I love that about travel, the twists and turns it can unexpectedly throw at you, serendipitous collisions and connections, moments in time and pure chance can provide massive highs as well as occasional challenges.

We had arrived in Bangkok the week before. We were all fighting fit again. Our plan was to spend a few days in the city, and then head up by sleeper train to the northern town of Chiang Mai. However, we discovered the train was sold out. What a stroke of luck. Our Cambodian side trip would never have happened if tickets had been available. We would have been away on the train, and perhaps never even known we had missed a golden opportunity to redeem my mathematical mistake.

Having established that there were cheap internal flights to Chiang Mai for the day after our return to Bangkok, we parted with £400 at the excursions desk. The following morning, after an early breakfast, we packed our bags for Siem Reap, the town where we would be based for our tour of Angkor Wat.

The journey itself was an experience. The first part was straightforward, five hours in a modern air-conditioned minibus along tarmac roads to the border. We arrived at a bustling market town full of colourful stalls selling exotic fruit, unusual vegetables and live animals. We snacked on noodles as we stood outside a food stall whilst our tour guide disappeared to purchase our visas. We tried not to be concerned that he was now in possession of our all-essential passports. Before too long, he returned and led us on foot to the border post. Relieved and excited, we smiled politely at the sombre customs officers, our passports were stamped, and we were on our way to Cambodia.

As we carried our hand luggage across the half mile-wide no man's land between the two countries, things became surreal. We had stumbled into a collection of casinos, entirely out of place but clearly popular even on a Tuesday lunchtime. Massive modern complexes with fountains, palm trees and grand facades, more Las Vegas than rural South-East Asia. We later discovered that gambling is illegal in both countries. People come here from far and wide to satisfy their passion, or maybe addiction. We had wondered why there were so many Thais at passport control without any luggage. They were day gamblers.

Stepping into what felt like a 19th-century American frontier town, we left behind Thailand's relatively westernised infrastructure. Suddenly this was replaced by muddy tracks for roads, clapped-out cars and more potholes than the surface of the moon. The four-hour long journey on the unconstructed road was hair-raising. A rally driver would have complained that conditions were too dangerous to proceed. Not our unfazed taxi driver though, slaloming his way through 150 kilometres worth of roadworks at great speed as we wound and bumped our way to Siem Reap.

Any trip like this is bound to include a built-in scam. They are usually minor and you can live with them, but this one nearly cost us £80, a significant chunk of our budget. Our handler at the border had advised us we needed to purchase Cambodian Riels because cashpoints would only dispense US Dollars which local traders would not accept. On our arrival in the modern and fast-expanding town of Siem Reap, we quickly discovered this was untrue. Everything was in Dollars.

The scam was based on the assumption that tourists would not know how many Riels they should get for their money. We were ripped off with a 40% commission rate of which any rogue trader would be proud. I was incandescent with rage. Or as we say in Scotland, I had the radge.

By the time I realised it was too late. However, once I calmed down, I had a light bulb moment. If we used the US dollars we carried for emergencies, it might be possible to change the Riels back at the border on our return journey to Bangkok. Unlikely but worth a try. I complained to the hotel manager.

"The rest of the tour package is excellent, and I would be happy to go online and recommend it to other travellers. But if this issue with the currency is not sorted, I will have to contact Lonely Planet and warn people not to use your hotel and this tour."

This cunning plan worked. We got our £80 back on our return to the border.

Our brief detour into Cambodia gave us a small insight into the impact of the atrocities waged on this beautiful country in the 1970s. The Khmer Rouge's murderous regime, led by their paranoid leader Pol Pot, destroyed Cambodian life for a generation. This psychotic despot was on a mission to create a Cambodian master race through social engineering, much like Hitler just 35 years previously. Two million people died, many executed as enemies of the state, others perished due to starvation, disease or overwork. As a student, I had watched an unsettling movie called *The Killing Fields*, and its chilling impact haunted me as we witnessed the aftermath of these true events three decades on.

However, this was a family trip. We had only recently visited Hiroshima. It would have been unfair to expose our children to so many horrors of history within such a short period of time. We decided that visiting museums full of graphic images, blood-curdling stories and human skulls might be a step too far. What could not be avoided however, was the age of the population around us. I was in my early forties, and rarely saw anyone older than me. If I did see anyone so ancient, they were invariably amputees. Now that was chilling, for me at least.

We had good reason to visit the ancient kingdom city of Angkor Wat, an enormous Buddhist temple complex, easily reached by tuk-tuk just five miles outside Siem Reap. It is one of the world's most impressive historical and photogenic sites.

Vast in scale, the ravages of time have been kind to many of its incredible buildings, and it was relatively easy to visualise it in its heyday. Even though the site welcomes some two million visitors each year, many of whom arrive early in the morning to capture images of the sunrise over this magical place, it was not overrun by hordes of tourists. There were however thousands of monkeys, swinging from temple to temple, like a scene from *The Jungle Book*.

Angkor Wat, or *temple city* in the Khmer language, was originally built in the 12th century as a Hindu temple. Sprawling over more than 400 acres, it is reputed to be the largest religious monument in the world even though it is no longer an active temple.

Over the centuries this temple complex slowly started to crumble. It was rediscovered in the 1840s by the French explorer Henri Mouhot, who wrote that the site was "*grander than anything left to us by Greece or Rome*." When Cambodia fell into a brutal civil war in the 1970s, Angkor Wat thankfully suffered minimal damage. However, the Khmer Rouge fought invading forces here during the Vietnam War, as testified by the pockmarks from bullets in the outer walls that sit just beyond the temple's moat.

Angkor Wat is the name of just one small part of the complex, albeit the best-known. What makes it so magical is its potent blend of history, culture, nature, beauty, water, symbolism and majesty. And the most fantastic light casting mystical shadows in and around the ancient ruins.

We were fortunate enough to pick a sunny day, arriving as the sun rose spectacularly overhead. The early morning sky was full of hot air balloons transporting tourists on the journey of a lifetime. I was happy to remain on terra firma on this occasion.

We stayed all day, hiring a tuk-tuk to take us from temple to temple. Our patience was rewarded as the sunset was unforgettable, and the photographs we took truly stunning.

What good fortune we had to be able to visit Angkor Wat after all.

Thailand
A hard drive

Before our Cambodian side trip, an unqualified success and redemption for the budget holder, we spent a busy few days in Bangkok. We had been warned this Asian metropolis would be chaotic, polluted and not particularly family-friendly. But that was not our experience. Hot and humid, yes. And, like any Asian city, we always had to be on our guard for scams.

With a treasure trove of exotic cultural sites available, we easily filled a few days. By basing ourselves near the backpacker hub of the world, the Khao San Road, we could access a wide choice of cool bars, cafés and street markets. At night-time, we kept away from the more lurid parts of this area, we were not the target market, and the bars did not offer the activities we were looking for. Enough said, if you catch my drift.

One of the best ways to travel around was along the Chao Phraya river, acting as the city's arteries, with the many river taxis binding the city together much as the Star Ferries did in Hong Kong harbour.

The Grand Palace in Bangkok is one of the most visited attractions in Asia. This large temple complex, full of iconography, gleaming spires and intricate carvings, was well worth the steep entrance fee. At a fifth of the price, we enjoyed just as much the Wat Po temple complex, famous for housing the world's largest reclining Buddha.

Continuing our tour of Bangkok's temples, we visited the Indiana Jones style Temple of the Dawn where we climbed impossibly steep steps for a bird's eye view of the city below.

Possibly our favourite temple was Golden Mount. A straightforward climb, at least early in the morning, this temple with a golden spire offered even better views of the Bangkok panorama and provided an ideal retreat from the urban heat and noise. We also loved the whimsically named Metal Castle, Loha Prasa. This one had metal spikes around the top and looked almost Japanese. By this stage of the trip, we were starting to compare places we had already visited.

Finally, we visited the world's largest solid gold Buddha, weighing a staggering five and a half tons. Three metres tall, this lustrous beauty was discovered by accident. Centuries previously, it had been covered with a layer of concrete mixed with sparkling glass in an attempt to conceal its true significance and protect it from thieves. It was moved several times over the years, before finally coming to Bangkok in the 20th century. Due to lack of space, the statue was stored in a basic building with a tin roof. Nobody realised its importance.

Eventually, a new building was constructed for the statue. It was accidentally damaged while being transported to its new home, revealing gold glinting through the concrete casing. This beautiful Buddha's real splendour emerged.

Imagine being that removal man coming home from work in the evening.

"Darling, I've got something to tell you," to be met by the retort, "Where have you been? You're late, your dinner's burnt."

An obvious Bangkok itinerary I guess, but one we enjoyed. I suspected one or more of us would return in the future. It is a great launching pad for this part of the world.

We concluded our Bangkok and bonus Cambodian experience, safe in the knowledge we had captured some of the best photos of the trip so far, memories we would be able to look back at for the rest of our lives. But we weren't done with Thailand just yet. It was time to visit the charms, sights and wildlife of the far north of Thailand.

We were often greeted at a new destination with the annoying words, "Oh, you should have been yesterday/last weekend because we had this amazing festival/parade/concert."

In the case of Northern Thailand's tourist epicentre, Chiang Mai, we fell lucky. Bang in the middle of our visit was the week-long annual Festival of Light, celebrating the end of the rainy season on November Full Moon. The town's whole complexion changed, with spectacular parades and street markets, fireworks, firecrackers, and colourful lanterns hung across every street. The festival is celebrated nationwide, but Chiang Mai is renowned as the best.

On Full Moon day itself, home-made hot air balloons made from what looked like stitched together IKEA bags were released into the air. Firecrackers and polystyrene planes were attached emitting coloured smoke trails like the Red Arrows.

We spent the afternoon making traditional floating offerings out of banana leaves and tropical flowers. Thousands of these beautiful *Krathong* sailed on the river at night, including, on this occasion, our own feeble efforts.

When darkness fell, we helped make fire lanterns, white paper-like cylinders with a paraffin-soaked cloth attached to the bottom along with firecrackers as pyromaniacal bonuses. A flame was lit and then inserted whilst participants held the lantern aloft. When it was hot enough, it was launched into the night sky. Us and thousands of other people took part in this visual extravaganza.

No environmental or safety assessments were carried out, and after a while, we moved back. But not until we had launched our lantern, and a ladle full of hot paraffin had poured itself onto poor Roonagh's arm. We were horrified and she was in floods of tears. Fortunately, no lasting harm was done. So much for health and safety.

But even without the Light Festival, Chiang Mai offered much for the visitor, and we made the most of it. There were plenty of choices.

One option was tiger petting. We decided against participating in such an ethically questionable activity as we knew that the animals were drugged and mistreated by their owners.

However, there was another indigenous animal we were much keener to meet, but only in the right way.

The story of the Asian Elephant in Thailand is a sad one. When the Thai Government introduced the commendable and correct policy of banning logging a few years ago, many working elephants were at a stroke made unemployed. Their owners, the mahouts, no longer had an income to maintain their hungry workers, and many became surplus to requirements. Abandonment and exploitation followed, the latter being the more common and profitable outcome.

Elephants soon became an integral part of Thailand's burgeoning tourist industry. Some begging in the streets of major cities, others providing elephant rides, such a popular component of treks and day trips. Elephant Parks trained these magnificent and intelligent beasts to do tricks for punters, including painting art which fetched thousands of dollars. We even saw one distressed and emaciated elephant chained up as a tourist attraction outside a Buddhist shrine, a terrible juxtaposition of religion and cruelty. Unfortunately for Thailand's elephant population, all these new forms of employment resulted in injury, either mental, physical or both. Mental trauma, broken legs from car accidents in cities or deformed spines from carrying overfed tourists on their backs in metal cages. There is no Trade Union for elephants.

Most visitors to Thailand are blissfully unaware of this sad story, and unwittingly perpetuate the injustice. How could they reasonably expect to know? A visit to the Elephant Nature Park near Chiang Mai is the answer. A remarkable place where injured elephants are treated and provided with a new home.

Set deep in the countryside, along a gently flowing river, paddy fields and deep green forest, this retreat was an idyllic setting to spend a few hours in the company of these awe-inspiring animals. We didn't just get to see them from afar, this was a hands-on experience.

On the way, we called in at a wholesale market and collected fruit, lots of it. It wasn't a huge surprise to find that juicy ripe bananas were the elephants' favourite as we hand fed them their mid-morning snack. The kids loved dropping fruit into their enormous mouths or waiting for an inquisitive trunk to appear and cheekily grab a banana from their hands.

After an educational session in our latest world classroom, where the kids learnt all about the challenges that elephant conservation faces, not least the cost of looking after these huge and hungry animals, it was bath time. Not for us, although at times it felt like it was. We walked down to the river, buckets and brushes in hand, together with a couple of dozen dirty elephants excitedly trumpeting on the way.

We soon set to work, filling up our buckets with water from the gently flowing river, and then tentatively approaching each elephant to give them a good scrub. I am not sure who enjoyed this more, the kids or the elephants. The latter were very grateful though, giving each of us a sloppy kiss on the cheek with their trunk. An elephant kisses like a vacuum cleaner sucks up dust, loud and dirty.

The next day, sat in the Elephant Café near our guest house, nursing a mango smoothie, I commenced my regular ritual of connecting to Wi-Fi to upload our many photos. My laptop suddenly made a nasty whirring noise, a circle started spiralling in the centre of the screen, and then it just went dead. Those bumpy rutted roads in Cambodia had taken their toll on its inner workings.

My heart stopped. I had foolishly wiped the memory card containing Bangkok and Cambodia's photos before they had uploaded. Not only was the laptop dead, but all those precious photographic mementoes were lost. I was devastated. It was heart-breaking, completely avoidable and all my own stupid fault. A few days later, we replaced the hard drive, but I had lost the photos for good. What an idiot.

We cheered ourselves up the following morning with some culinary therapy. Much like elephant trips, there were hundreds of options for Thai cookery classes. Eventually, we found an organic farm and vegetarian cooking experience. After an early morning market stop, where we procured perfectly perfumed herbs and spices, we headed to a small farm half an hour outside Chiang Mai. Following a tour of the carefully drilled rows of various exotic vegetables and orchards full of fruit trees, we were taken into a large sweaty kitchen, provided with aprons and conical hats and the lesson commenced.

After expert instruction, we set to work. It was like Thai Masterchef. We prepared a wide array of Thai classics such as spring rolls, papaya salad, green and red curry and mango ice cream. Quite a feast, enough to fill our rumbling stomachs and still have enough leftovers for a carry-out for our evening meal. Feeling like Michelin-starred chefs, we left proudly clutching the recipe booklet with great plans for future family cooking experiences. It has languished untouched in our Scottish kitchen ever since.

Occasionally in your life, a special day comes along which you will never forget. There are those punctuation marks in life, of course, like your first day at school, first kiss, wedding day and the birth of your children. Then there are days when you just think, *Wow, did that really happen to me, how lucky and blessed I am.* Those days that make you grateful for the life you have.

Family travel comes with stresses and strains. 24/7 living, moving all the time and the ever-present shadow of the trip budget. Missing home, family and friends and nagging worries about what will happen when you return home, especially if you happen to travel during a global recession. But it wouldn't have been an adventure without challenges, and an adventure is what we were having.

All of this meant that special, never to be forgotten, moments were even more precious. We had experienced more than our fair share already. You might be sick or insanely jealous of all the fabulous things we had done, places we had been to and the experiences we had. If so, then, don't read on. Because when we did an eco-trek to a Thai Hill Tribe deep in the Golden Triangle sandwiched between Thailand, Laos and Myanmar, we had not just one never to be forgotten day, but three.

In Chiang Mai, there were a plethora of tourist agencies offering tours to Hill Tribe Villages. All included elephant riding and bamboo rafting. Some claimed to be *eco* with little or no explanation as to what this meant. Only one operator offered an authentic eco-experience, and we were fortunate enough to stumble upon them. A company whimsically called *Pooh's Eco Tours*. We didn't meet Mr Pooh, although we were assured that he existed, not just in the Hundred Acre Wood. But we did encounter his best friend, Mr Tee, who came from a Karen Tribe and spent his time taking small groups of westerners on visits into his world. This excursion was designed to enrich all parties and have a minimal environmental impact.

After a three-hour transfer riding high in the back of a roofless truck, we made our way on foot to the Po Karen Hill Tribe village where we were to spend our first night. We were welcomed into a one-room home on stilts, where we slept outside on a wooden platform under a mosquito net. Hogs snorted below our thin mattresses. Night-time toilet trips to the hole in the ground, which had been dug earlier that day in our honour, took place under a spectacular starry sky.

The Hill Tribes live a simple, subsistence-based life. Everything is organic. They will hunt and eat anything, including grabbing frogs out of the sand by the river for their tea. The village housed 117 families, a total of over 500 people.

The vast majority of the villagers still followed traditional beliefs, and each community had a witchdoctor. I say "*witchdoctor*" for that is what Mr Tee called him, rather than the less pejorative term *shamen*.

Twenty families had recently converted to Christianity. Mexican missionaries had built a church which was the grandest building in the entire area.

Intrigued to meet this strange, white-skinned family, the villagers were friendly and hospitable. Mr Tee ran the only tour visiting this area. He explained that he engaged help from different villagers each time he brought a group, meaning the income was shared equally. This was authentic communal living. Everyone helped everybody else, everyone was a cousin or brother. Not literally though, we were assured they were careful about that. Content with their lot, life expectancy was high. We were surprised to see quite a few octogenarians, all in fantastic nick.

Mr Tee told us he only takes a family with children to the village once a year. A red-haired boy and a blonde girl were quite an attraction. Their new friends soon whisked them off and Rory enjoyed his first football game in five months. Roonagh played hopscotch and the village girls presented her with bouquets of wildflowers. The kids' digital cameras and sunglasses were also a great attraction. Language was no barrier to fun.

After our night's sleep in the open, we headed off for a tour of the village. A valuable insight into their way of life: hunting, religion, births, marriage and death. We met one lady making a wedding dress for her marriage in three days' time to a man from a neighbouring village she had met one week previously. Her elderly prospective mother-in-law assisted at the wooden loom while smoking her pipe. All the women smoked pipes. Given their life expectancy, perhaps smoking isn't as bad for your health as we think. Or maybe they used special life-enhancing tobacco.

We trekked through stunning scenery. Very tropical, but fortunately not too hot nor humid. The villagers whose turn it was to help this western family were brilliant, especially with the kids. Rory walked the whole way with the fantastically named *Papa Monkey*, not his real name I suspect. Roonagh rode piggyback nearly all the time. This was particularly helpful given we had to cross several rivers at adult waist height. Arriving at a riverside wooden hut, we took a refreshing dip in the chilly waters whilst tea was prepared on the open fire. Utensils, plates and even a teapot were expertly fashioned from freshly foraged bamboo.

After a delicious Thai supper, we settled down on the hut's floor for a surprisingly good night's sleep. The following morning's breakfast included campfire chips, setting us up nicely for fantastic, albeit challenging, hiking. We headed upstream for a couple of hours, literally. This was proper river walking.

Next stop was the *Bat Cave*, a gargantuan cavern the river surged through. Just as our guides were preparing their flame torches, they spotted a three-metres long snake on a rock ledge. A couple of slingshots later the serpent was dispatched, and no doubt featured on that evening's menu.

We made our way through the 180-metres long cave, pitch dark except for the flickering light of the torches. We had just one tumble between us and made it to the other side before the torches burnt through.

A couple of hours later, after more walking and a lunch stop, the truck took us back to Chiang Mai. Exhausted yet exhilarated, the three hour journey back to our hotel flew by. We all made a hasty path to the shower for a good scrub down. When I came out of the bathroom, I found both kids face down, prostrate on the tiled floor, fast asleep with their heads on their daysacks. I scooped them up, laid them in their beds, and we retired for the night, happy but tired campers.

The next evening, we boarded the night train back to Bangkok. Sleep was not to be found in our four-bed compartment and the first-class toilets were to be avoided at all cost. We arrived back in the Thai capital at dawn and found a hotel that would rent a room for the morning to store our bags.

After breakfast and a cold shower, we jumped in a tuk-tuk for a whistle-stop tour of the city, this time with the sole objective of recreating our lost photos.

Mission accomplished, the kids happily watched *The Bee Movie* in the airport taxi's DVD player as we headed to the final chapter of our Asian adventure, Singapore.

Singapore
Bad timing

Like so many who make the journey from Europe to Australia, we had a stopover in Singapore. Four nights in one of the most expensive countries in the world.

We only just made it to this most modern of South East Asian city states. As we left Bangkok, Thailand was gripped with political protests. For once, our timing was impeccable. The day after we flew out of Bangkok, the airport was taken over by thousands of riotous rebels who could have scuppered our plans. Who knows what might have happened then, maybe something even better?

At the crossroads of Asia and the West, both geographically and historically, the Republic of Singapore has the world's second largest population density. Sophisticated and modern, this is a strategically important maritime nation and one of the world's leading financial centres.

Sir Stamford Raffles founded Singapore in 1819 as a trading post for the British Empire. We walked past the grand colonial hotel named after him one sticky afternoon, melting in the city's heat and humidity, longing for a *Singapore Sling*, the gin-based cocktail famously served in the hotel's bar.

We didn't enjoy Singapore. I am sorry, but there you have it. Maybe it was the contrast with the subsistence-based living we had just experienced in the Thai Hill Tribe where people had nothing but seemed so content and fulfilled. Here it was all about the dollar. It felt uncomfortable, almost distasteful, and we weren't quite ready to move on from such a profoundly spiritual experience.

I have already explained that how you feel about a place sometimes comes down to how you feel about yourself. The first time I visited Kandy in Sri Lanka on holiday I didn't like it. I was tired, grumpy and out of my comfort zone. It felt bothersome, claustrophobic and overwhelming. Two years later, living in Sri Lanka as a volunteer, it became my go-to place for the weekend.

In business, there is a saying *Above and Below the Line*. If something goes wrong, you have a choice. You can go *below the line* and blame someone else, make excuses or deny it happened at all. Or you can go *above the line* and take ownership of the situation, accountability for its success or failure and responsibility for fixing it.

During our short time in Singapore, I am afraid I fell below the line. How I was feeling was all my fault, yet I was in denial, blaming the city rather than my own emotions. The kids were fine though, they loved being back in so-called civilization.

It is not as if we stayed in the heart of the Financial District or a five-star hotel. We based ourselves in the Little India area, mainly because, whilst still expensive, it was nearly affordable to stay there. This also allowed us to say a fond farewell to Asia.

The area was stereotypically Indian, at 5:00 pm the streets thronged with men of all ages, smoking and drinking. Not a woman to be seen, they were no doubt at home preparing the evening meal and tending the young folk.

It was the end of November, and to be fair, Singapore does Christmas well. Much better than Australia as we were soon to discover. There were decorations and twinkling lights everywhere. This felt surreal coming out of perpetual summer. What happened to autumn?

We took a spin on the Singapore Flyer, the largest Ferris Wheel in Asia, for views across the city, the bay and into Malaysia. And celebrity spotted Orchid specimens planted at the Botanical Gardens over the years by famous names such as Nelson Mandela, Margaret Thatcher and Diana, Princess of Wales.

As we enjoyed our final supper in Asia, five months into our travels and about to enter Oceania, we reflected on so many adventures, so much laughter and how tight a unit the Family Trippers now were. Putting all our scrapes to one side, the trip was going remarkably well. We were back on budget and had just had the best five months of our lives. There were still seven to go.

Goodbye Asia, Hello Australia.

Western Australia
Chilly nights and sunny days

After two months under African skies and three months criss-crossing the charms of East and South East Asia, we arrived for three months in Australia. A far-off land only previously glimpsed through the stereotypes emanating from our television screens. Oz, the land of Kylie, Jason and Skippy. Down Under, where the women are called Sheila, the blokes are blokes and everyone's your mate.

My first thought when I dreamt of Australia was the heat. Long hot days. Balmy nights. Maybe humid, perhaps the occasional shower, but certainly heat. Real heat. Especially in December as another British winter was beginning to bite 9,000 miles away.

As we sweated in the Tropics the kids kept hearing, "Just you wait till Australia, then you'll really have something to whinge about." And Anne kept hearing, "I can't wait for that pint of cold Aussie lager, I can almost taste it already."

There are dreams and then reality. Some days were like a good English summer, the daytime weather was mixed. Others like a typical Scottish summer day, cold and rainy. Night-time was distinctly nippy. On occasions positively, but not quite literally, freezing.

Seven weeks Asian budget accommodation traded for an Aussie adventure under canvas. We thought we were taking the easy option. We wanted to ensure the kids, and to be frank their parents, enjoyed not just endured the experience. Home comforts, hassle-free time and chilling out in more familiar surroundings.

First up, a couple of nights in Perth, Western Australia, the most remote city in the world. Unless you live there in which case, I guess it is the most accessible city in the world.

Having checked into our hotel, we dashed to the nearest pub for that cold pint of Aussie Lager. It was 30th November, St Andrew's Day. The bar had a themed promotion and the guest ale was Belhaven Best, brewed just one mile from our Scottish home. The lager could wait. What were the chances? "Who had had the easier journey us or the beer?" I asked Anne rhetorically. It was the smoothest and sweetest pint of my life. The kids had J2o juices and were just as happy.

The next day, we collected our hire vehicle for a month-long Western Australia road trip, taking the suburban train from Perth to Stirling. Home from home.

We headed up north with a pair of two-person tents, air beds and a pump. We were sure we would be fine with the mummy liners we had brought. It was an Australian summer, after all. Wrong. Incorrect. We shivered through our first two nights, even with multiple clothing layers.

After the first bone-chilling and teeth-chattering night, the kids spent the next three in the car. Suffice to say we were the proud owners of four new sleeping bags before the week was out.

Excited at being in Australia, I decided we should play our own version of *I spy*. "There's a prize for the first person to spot a kangaroo," I announced, as we left the low-rise suburban outskirts of Perth. It didn't take long for the kids to grow bored of this facile attempt at in-car entertainment. They soon settled into playing with their Nintendo DS, their default mobile entertainment portals on many long travel hours.

This deceptively addictive diversion proved well-timed. Sure enough, we did see a kangaroo at the side of the road and I won the prize. But it remained unclaimed and unexplained. Our first kangaroo sighting was roadkill. Not the first Skippy I had hoped to see.

If Salvador Dali drank Carling and then built sandcastles, he did so in the dramatic Pinnacles in Nambung National Park, three hours north of Perth. The best time to visit these geological stunners was sunset. The intense summer sun dipped above and beyond the multitudes of sandstone pillars scattered spectacularly across the golden desert floor. Fantastical shapes and eerie shadows danced in every direction. The kids loved climbing these unique structures, some up to five metres high. Posing for photos and playing *Hide and Seek* much more successfully than our attempt at *I Spy*.

Distances in Western Australia were deceptively long, particularly for us *Poms* from such a relatively tiny country. What looked like a short hop on the map could take half a day or more. I had to be careful to keep the petrol tank filled up for fear of being stranded in the middle of nowhere. On more than one occasion we were rescued by petrol stations that looked like they only opened every third Wednesday in a month that did not include the letter a.

Heading south and then inland, our next stop was Perth Hills National Park. On the way, we discovered there was no Sunday shopping in Perth. More nights without sleeping bags.

The Christmas holidays were yet to start. We were the only people staying in the camping area, giving us exclusive access to the outdoor kitchen, many mobs of kangaroos and colourful birdlife.

Our first week's third and final stop was the Porongorup Hills Range 50 kilometres from the south coast. We managed to get sleeping bags on the way, to everyone's relief.

We planned to stay for a couple of nights until a mishap befell our camping gear and undid this cunning plan. The poles for one of the tents snapped upon arrival. The next morning, after a fun night of all four trippers in one wee tent, the second tent broke.

Confession time. I said in the opening chapter of this book that I sometimes sanitised our blogs. Here is a classic example. Yes, the tent pole did break. But only after Anne and I had a huge row, my fault entirely. The exhaustion of long-distance driving taking its toll on my tolerance levels. She ended up sleeping in the car whilst my well-deserved punishment was to sleep in the tiny tent with the kids.

I would love to say this was our final tent related disagreement. In truth, the kids learnt to retreat to a safe distance every time it was tent assembly time. They knew what was coming. It was all my bad. Apart from when it wasn't.

The south-west corner of the last country before Antarctica is a beautiful and diverse land. Mountains, lakes, giant trees, balmy beaches, waterfalls, gorges, blowholes, rock formations, vineyards and much more. Like a condensed version of the whole of Europe, there is even a town called Denmark.

We arrived in Albany with no functioning tents and our energy reserves somewhat depleted. The distinctly Scottish weather and coal grey skies did little to give us an initial burst of adrenalin. Albany was one of those places which falls short when you come across it first time around. But we hung around and waited for the sun to come out. It proved to be an excellent introduction to this part of the world. Most travellers come here last on the south-west loop. We decided to travel in reverse, going against the flow. It worked for us.

Before we left home, we wanted to ensure that we didn't just experience places through hotels. We were keen to have the opportunity to meet people in real-life situations and understand how they lived. One way to do this was through an organisation called SERVAS.

SERVAS is a worldwide network of people who are committed to spreading peace and understanding through face-to-face contact. I am pleased to see they have survived the global dominance of Airbnb. The deal is that the host, if willing and able, provides two nights' accommodation to the SERVAS traveller. No money changes hands, but both parties hopefully benefit by exchanging experiences, information and ideas.

We ended up staying three nights in Albany with a friendly middle-aged man called Steve. The kids enjoyed playing with his two daughters, and he gave us free use of their bikes, together with helpful tips on the best places to go and things to see. Steve and his family had recently spent six months travelling around Europe in a camper van, so it was great to spend time with like-minded folk. Rather worryingly, he and his wife had just separated, blaming the stresses of travelling in close proximity for exposing the pre-existing tensions in their relationship. It seemed like a good time for us to buy a larger tent. This time a proper family tent with a lounge and two bedrooms. You get what you pay for.

Albany and the surrounding coastline reminded me of Cornwall in the south-west of England and the Cape of Good Hope in South Africa. These are both positive comparisons. Typical us though, I was the only family member to have been to both, Cornwall being the setting for many family holidays in my childhood. The rest of the tribe had only been to the comparator on the other side of the world. We often joke that the place in Scotland we go on holiday to most often is Edinburgh Airport. Which is crazy, we live in a beautiful country in its own right.

Our visit to Albany's Whaling Station was an eye-opening, environmental and educational experience. Set in a former Whaling Ship and Factory, mercifully not operational since the 1970s when the Australian Government finally banned commercial whaling, this museum taught us all about the whaling process, in all its bloody, gory details. As vegetarians, this was one of our more uncomfortable experiences so far. Sometimes it is good to learn about these practices, if only to remind us why we abhor them.

The next stop after Albany was just an hour down the road, the picturesque and relaxing town of Denmark. We pitched our new tent, at the Rivermouth Caravan Park, set perfectly by, yes, the river mouth. A glorious setting where, for once, there were no tent related arguments.

Travelling under canvas suited us. We had the freedom to choose where we stayed, and for how long. If we didn't like a place, we could just keep going. If we fancied it, we could linger a little longer. The kids enjoyed their freedom to roam, having been on a tight leash of safety for so long in Asia. Even if they did get many dirty looks from adults during the school week. "Why aren't those children in school?" we would hear whispered as we walked past.

The fresh air was revitalising, we were indulging in readily available western foods and quenching our thirst with delightful wine. We were back in holiday of a lifetime mode, much like in South Africa all those months ago, but this time with more travel experience, a tighter family bond and a flexible schedule.

Besides the joys of hanging out by the river and indulging in some delicious *Barbies*, we enjoyed two main activities. Firstly, a wine and cheese driving tour, including the Denmark Farmhouse Cheese tasting extravaganza. The sign said, "*Enjoy our cheese but don't make a meal of it.*" Sorry, but we did.

The second highlight was a dip in the waters of the picturesque Green Pool at Williams Bay National Park. If you are ever in this remote part of Western Australia, check it out. We also had a surreal Scottish Trippers moment, arriving at an outdoor market in the December sunshine to hear the strains of bagpipes performing Christmas Carols.

From Denmark, we headed to the vertiginous Valley of the Giants. A 40 metres high metal walkway right up to the top of the tree line. It recreated the feeling of being in the trees and therefore swayed up to 1.5 metres. The kids loved being up high with the birds and leaves. The look of enjoyment on their faces, together with the distraction of many photo opportunities, kept me going. Anne felt seasick.

Emboldened by my achievement in surviving this walk in the sky, the next tripper challenge for the guy who has suffered from vertigo all his life was to climb the 60 metres high Gloucester Tree. 143 terror-inducing steps later I made it, demonstrating what Anne christened "*Tripper Spirit.*" She came up with this phrase early in the trip to encapsulate the resilience and positivity we would sometimes need to dig deep to find when facing challenges or setbacks. Sometimes we would flip it to persuade the kids to do something they didn't want to, saying, "Come on kids, let's show some tripper spirit." Occasionally they would flip it back to us, "Oh come on Daddy, where's your Tripper Spirit?" Either way, it carried us through some sticky situations, and on occasions pushed us to embrace opportunities that were a wee bit scary.

This forest is home to three kinds of Tingle Tree, including the rare Red Tingle, the world's second-largest tree, only found in this small area. It is unusual because it does not have a tap root, rather a shallow root system spreading out around the tree which can be easily damaged. It also has a soft core, resulting in a massive hole in the lower portion of the otherwise healthy tree. These holes are great, you could park a car or have a small party in them.

On to the very end of the Australian continent and the small town of Augusta, from where the Southern Oceans stretch over 5,000 kilometres to the Antarctic. Due south was Argentina. For these Scots in the heat, the bracing maritime climate was ideal.

Our campsite sat gloriously at the head of the Blackwood River, nestled behind dunes to protect it from the ocean breeze.

Dolphins, cormorants and pelicans were plentiful. "Pellys" soon became my favourite bird in the world. And they had fierce competition. The birdlife of Australia is immense, the diversity of parrots and lorikeets being a constant source of enjoyment for us all.

Bird spotting became another amusement activity for the kids. It was a perfect spot to chill out, watch nature float or fly by, stroll on the long sandy beach or take a kayak out at sunset to shoot the breeze with the dolphins. We ended up staying twice as long as we had planned.

The largest show cave in Western Australia is the cavernous Jewel Cave. The calcite formations are probably some of the best anywhere and it is not too tacky. No coloured lights or music, just a guide and a small number of helpful observations like "and this stalactite looks like a chicken" or "this stalagmite is a dead ringer for Kylie."

The cave was discovered earlier last century through an opening in the ground formed by the decayed taproot of a massive Karri Tree. This tree, common in Western Australia and another giant, does have a tap root as long as the tree itself, and it was fun to see one breaking through the cave ceiling and reaching the floor of the first, higher cavern. Another excursion proving how the world could be a better teacher than the classroom, at least for pre-teens.

Augusta is in one of Australia's best wine growing regions, Margaret River. There were many wineries to visit. "Just catch up on your diaries kids, we won't be long." You can imagine their grumpy faces. Well, they were at school after all, so fair's fair.

Further up the south-west coast of Western Australia was Busselton Jetty. It is the longest jetty in the Southern Hemisphere at nearly two kilometres long. Imagine Blackpool Pier and just keep going. Like a giant Toblerone stretching out into the Indian Ocean. It's just loads of planks of wood nailed together really, but a great spot to stretch your legs whilst eating a fast-melting ice cream in the midday sun.

We based ourselves in Busselton for a couple of nights but not because of the jetty. That was a walk in the park, or should I say, *"walk on the water,"* compared to what we planned to do. The real reason we were here was because it was only 40 minutes' drive to Bunbury, one of the best places in Western Australia to swim with those most intelligent and graceful of marine mammals, dolphins.

First up was the opportunity to dip our toes in Bunbury's warm waters and meet a couple of local celebrities, dolphins called Levy and her pal Tangles, so-called because she had lost most of her fin, entangled in and slowly severed by a fishing line. Many dolphins are distinguishable by scars on their dorsal fins, caused either by sharks, by fighting or playing with other dolphins, or by the carelessness of earth's greatest predator, man.

One of the biggest dangers to dolphins, and other marine animals such as turtles, is discarded plastic. David Attenborough hadn't told the world this yet when we chatted with Levy and Tangles. We all know that now.

The kids couldn't believe what they were about to experience. Not only were they going to see dolphins, they were going to swim with them. We all excitedly jumped on board a converted fishing boat which took us out to the edge of the bay. It wasn't long until the boat slowed and then dropped anchor. We then had the tricky task of getting into our wetsuits, apart from Rory, who seemed a little out of sorts. I squeezed myself into mine, a bag of $5 chips at Augusta had started to have an impact on my waistline. Either that or I had erroneously been given a children's wetsuit.

We listened attentively to the obligatory safety demonstration and learnt the difference between interaction and interference. It turns out that if dolphins swim towards you, it is interaction. If they swim away, it is potentially damaging and stressful interference. So don't chase them. It took our minds back four months to the dramas of the armada-like dolphin cruise in Mauritius where we got this so badly wrong.

We were somewhat disappointed and slightly perturbed, to be told that there would be low underwater visibility due to stormy weather out at sea. This explained the rolling of the boat and Anne's puce-green face.

Allegedly there were dolphins down there, just like there were allegedly whales in South Africa. Our instructor explained that, even if we couldn't see any dolphins, we should be able to hear them talk to each other. So fully instructed and with snorkels at the ready, we jumped into the murky waters.

I am not sure whether it was dolphins I heard or the sound of my own heavy breathing as I struggled to stay afloat in the choppy waves. Roonagh claimed to have heard a dolphin whistling. I don't know if she really did, but if she believed she did, that's good enough for me. We swam around as best we could for 20 minutes with not a dolphin in sight before we had to admit the obvious and quit. I didn't want to, but we had to concede defeat.

Beaten and bedraggled, defeated and dejected, we hauled ourselves back into the boat. Would we ever have a trip out to sea that delivered what it said on the tin? We were beginning to doubt it. Every time we paid good money to go and see marine life, we were left disappointed. No matter, we could at least say we had been whale spotting and swimming with dolphins. The lack of actual sightings was just small print in the margins of our travel story. That's what I told the downhearted kids at least, but inside I was gutted.

Back in Busselton, we had some domestic issues to deal with. Poor Rory was feeling unwell with a stomach upset, which explained his strange mood onboard the boat. We upgraded to a caravan for a couple of nights so he could recuperate. Beds, a kitchen, a TV and the thing we desired most, our own toilet.

This luxury was an excuse for us to watch the start of an Australia vs South Africa cricket match. Four days later, Rory and I attended the final day's play at the WACA in Perth. For a lifelong cricket fan bringing up his son in Scotland, it was awesome to be able to catch some high-level international cricket at such a historic venue.

There was another reason why we upgraded our accommodation. We felt safer in the caravan, and it had its own fridge.

As campers under canvas, we needed to use the communal on-site fridge, and all our provisions, especially the beer and cheese, walked. We were fairly sure who had taken them, a dodgy looking solo male traveller just across the field who was clearly high on something. Given his was the only other tent in the campsite you didn't need to be Hercule Poirot to work that one out.

There was another safety-related reason for upgrading our accommodation, a secret reason only I knew about. This related to deadly spiders. That same evening, when Anne stood up to go to the communal kitchen, I lifted her chair, quickly and surprisingly coolly, carried it to the edge of the campsite, and shook off a venomous Redback spider. I decided to keep this anecdote to myself until we left Australia two months later. I was starting to form the impression that Australia might be beautiful, but not without its dangers as well.

We were done with life under canvas, at least for now. Our penultimate stop was the seaside town of Rockingham, a couple of hours further up the coast, before we headed back to Perth. We upgraded from a caravan to a sea view apartment, with separate bedrooms and carpet. The height of luxury. We all thought, *Thank you Rory for still feeling ill*, but did not dare say it to the poor lad.

One afternoon, leaving Anne to re-pack our bags in peace, Roonagh to write her diary and Rory to recuperate, I headed to a local internet café to upload the latest blog. I was excited to receive our first piece of fan mail. A family in Perth was planning to travel around the world, were following our journey through our blogs, and knew we were in Western Australia. They wanted to meet us. How exciting, we were famous. Well maybe not famous, but certainly ever so slightly flattered. Our egos gently massaged, we spent an enjoyable afternoon at their home a few days later on Anne's birthday. They even baked a cake for her. A small gesture, but it meant the world to her and us.

Anne's birthday is four days before Christmas, always a challenge for her unimaginative husband when it comes to presents. Roonagh is a massive fan of Christmas and still believed in Santa, or so she said, so we had to be creative in ensuring our festive traditions could still take place in the sunshine. Christmas Day is her favourite day of the year. By a distance. But it just didn't feel like Christmas.

We were nearly six months in, halfway around the world and homesickness hit Anne and the kids. Rather like marathon runners after 20 miles, they hit the wall. Backpacking in the developing world, whilst tiring at times, felt like backpacking. Whenever we returned to the western world, where there were shops, restaurants and home comforts that our budget would not allow us to enjoy fully, they missed being back home.

In Australia, we sat on many benches eating butties for lunch rather than dining in lovely cafés. Now we were in the sunshine, on the other side of the world, when it was supposed to be Christmas. It didn't feel festive at all.

An Aussie Christmas, at least in Western Australia, is very different from one back home. Yes, it's sunny, and yes they shop a lot, but nothing like in The UK. Let's face it, when it comes to a commercially focused Yuletide, we Brits rock. But here, on the other side of the world, there were hardly any Christmas lights in the streets. Perhaps because it didn't turn dark until 9:00 pm, compared to 3:30 pm in Scotland. Either way, it wasn't easy to get our heads around the fact this was Christmas. But we gave it a good go.

I wanted to make sure that we stayed somewhere special for Anne's birthday and Christmas. Extensive online research led to me booking a luxury apartment in Freemantle, 30 minutes south of Perth. It turned out that the agency managing this mouldy and poorly maintained box flat employed the world's most talented photographer. It looked nothing like the photos, more Mandela Towers in *Only Fools and Horses* than Santa's Grotto.

Undeterred, we headed to a nearby Dollar Store and splashed out $7 on a fake tree, tinsel and decorations. This attempt at festive fun may have been a poor effort by our usual standards, but Roonagh enjoyed making the flat as Christmassy as she could.

A couple of evenings later, Santa did visit our apartment, delivering a small but perfectly formed pile of practical or edible presents beneath the plastic tree, all lovingly wrapped in tinfoil.

The next morning, Christmas Day, was an occasion we needed to make memorable, especially for the kids.

After our traditional mince pie breakfast, and the opening of the bacofoil wrapped delights Santa had delivered, we drove under azure skies to the beautiful Yanchep National Park. It was 23 degrees with a slight breeze. About 17 degrees cooler than the previous year's Christmas Day in Perth, thank goodness. And 15 degrees warmer than back home.

We chose Yanchep because we knew there would be plenty to keep homesick minds occupied. We headed straight to the Koala enclosure to wish the residents Merry Christmas. These adorable marsupials were pretty sleepy, perhaps they had already been on the Sherry. They were scheduled to line their stomachs with eucalyptus leaves later on for Christmas Dinner. We received a lesson in all things Koala and learnt that eucalyptus contains a poisonous toxin which is fatal unless the koala has certain bacteria in its gut. They are not born with these bacteria. When the ever so cute Baby Koalas are weaned at about six months, they must eat their mother's excrement. That nearly put me off my Christmas Dinner.

After a rather pathetic attempt at making a boomerang come back to us, we attended a demonstration about the traditional aboriginal people, the Noongar. This was a fascinating insight into their life, learning about plants they used, how they made fire, how they hunted and cared for the land, and how to do a simple aboriginal dot drawing. To the kids' great amusement, their mortified parents were dragged up to learn an aboriginal dance. Probably no more complicated than the Hokey Cokey, I'm not sure we were naturals, but we gave it a whirl. It was Christmas Day after all. Apparently.

It was now time for our Christmas Day Dinner. I must confess that despite our best efforts, it wasn't our most delicious attempt ever. I had prepared skewers containing parsnips, carrots and sprouts to sit alongside our veggie sausages and hash browns. The vegetables were somewhat undercooked, and the meal preparation took longer than usual due to the temperamental BBQ we were using. But we entered into the spirit of things at least. After a short rest to digest our food, we had a game of cricket, sporting our Christmas party hats, much to the amusement of the locals.

On our way back to Freemantle for a delicious plate of Camembert and Christmas Cake, we stopped off at a rather breezy beach for a quick festive splash in the water. I'm sure the Aussies thought we were mad. Obviously *Poms,* we were virtually the only people wearing Christmas gear. But we made an effort. When you're the other side of the world, and feeling every mile from home, you have to go for it and enjoy.

We learnt a couple of valuable lessons in Freemantle. Firstly, when you are staying in a new place, make sure you check out both directions, turn left as well as right. One evening we fancied a barbecue. We had seen public BBQs in parks in every Australian town so far. We jumped in the car and drove around.

An hour later we gave up and took our veggie burgers back to the flat. The next morning, I went for a walk. I turned left outside the front door rather than taking my usual route to the right. There, 50 metres away, was a small park with a BBQ. From that point on, wherever we stayed, we made sure we explored to the left of our base as well as to the right.

Another valuable lesson, particularly in this part of the world, was to ask locals why no-one was in the sea on a hot summer's day. We headed to one of the best beaches in the area, Cottesloe, colloquially known as *Cotto*. We arrived, fully swim suited, towels in hand, ready for a plunge in the warm waters. The beach was busy, but there was no one in the sea. There were helicopters overhead which seemed a little strange.

"Woah mate, where do you think you're going?" shouted a concerned lifeguard as we charged into the shallows. It turned out there had been a fatal shark attack just an hour before, and the search for the deadly Great White was in full flow. Suitably shocked, we quickly turned around and went to buy ice cream instead, a much safer bet.

A few ice creams later, with Christmas in the sunshine done and dusted, it was time to leave Western Australia and head to the East Coast for the annual celebration Scots do best, Hogmanay. Where better to experience New Year than Sydney Harbour?

New South Wales & Victoria Parties, penguins and plans

Sydney was exactly what we expected. I don't know if that is a good thing or not, but it was strangely familiar.

Maybe it was because we had seen photos of it so many times.

Maybe it was because we had heard many stories about it from friends, including the couple whose home we stayed in for this leg of the trip.

Maybe it was because it was a clean western city and felt like it could have been in Europe or the USA.

Whatever the reason, we settled in quickly and took in the sights.

Sydney is massive. With only a few days at our disposal, it was impossible to see everything, and at times we were not sure we really understood the city's layout. The impressive public transport network helped though, including the flotillas of ferries down by the Opera House transporting locals and tourists alike across the bay in many different directions.

One ferry took us to the ANZ Stadium, venue for the 2000 Olympic Games and England's dramatic last kick win against Australia in the 2003 Rugby World Cup Final. We were looking forward to a tour and to follow in the footsteps of Cathy Freeman, Haile Gebrselassie and Jonny Wilkinson. But just like in Yokohama, my sport-related research let me down and we arrived shortly after closing time.

We had always dreamt of being in Sydney for New Year's Eve and watching the fireworks over the Harbour Bridge. Australia's most iconic image, the Opera House, floodlit whilst a symphony of fireworks would explode to a thumping soundtrack amid gasps of awe and wonder from the assembled throng. Topping it all, this year's display promised to be the biggest and best ever. Over 5,000 tonnes of fireworks were due to be launched in 12 scintillating minutes.

There were many different vantage points around the harbour area and beyond to watch the display. The friends we were staying with had warned us that we would have to arrive early whichever we chose. Mind you, not quite as early as those who had set up camp at teatime the day before outside the Opera House.

We also had some key criteria for our choice of location. A great view, of course, and close to public transport links to enable a quick and safe getaway after the festivities had ended. Also, somewhere that would be family-friendly, meaning stewards would control access and the kids would not feel too claustrophobic in the crowds. And perhaps most importantly, revellers would not consume alcohol in such large quantities that it would spoil the atmosphere for us. In the end, four out of five wasn't bad, but not quite good enough.

Ian Pilbeam

We arrived at Blue Point Reserve nice and early, just before noon. Our first view of Sydney Harbour and the Opera House was breath-taking. It was like looking at a giant photograph in a travel agency window. We pitched camp at a pretty much perfect position, the centre of the Bridge bang on 12 o'clock, clockface speaking.

And then the long wait. The kids were on their best behaviour, doing loads of schoolwork. What a great setting for a classroom. We rigorously applied sun cream, although several applications of Factor 50 still didn't prevent Rory's young Scottish skin from burning. We hydrated well, with copious amounts of water.

Meanwhile, all around us, alcohol brought in before the midday security checks was steadily being consumed, and then the bar opened at 4:00 pm. By 6:00 pm the Portaloo area was becoming rather congested and unpleasant.

At 9:00 pm the Family Fireworks exploded into action, a taster for the main event, set to a soundtrack of family favourite tunes. Unfortunately, there were no speakers at our vantage point, so we couldn't hear the music. The fireworks were impressive though, especially in this setting. Ironically, we were surrounded by Scots. No doubt Edinburgh was full of Aussies celebrating Hogmanay. It's a topsy turvy world, so many people so far from home.

By this point, we figured it was no longer a family-friendly atmosphere. With a heavy heart, we made the sensible parental decision to head home, which proved to be the correct choice. New Year's Eve in Sydney is no different than Edinburgh or London, it's very lively. Whilst it was a fab party atmosphere, the kids were 10 years too young and we were 20 years too old.

We ended up watching the midnight fireworks on the TV back at our friends' house, stepping out onto the front porch to hear the bangs echoing across the Sydney sky.

Maybe we have some unfinished business for later in our lives, but at least we have been to Sydney's New Year celebrations once.

When we woke up the next morning, it was still last year back home. When the midnight bells rang in Edinburgh in minus 3 degrees temperature, and the bagpipes played out Auld Lang Syne, we were sweating on a veranda listening to BBC Radio Scotland, looking at the cloudless sky and 30 degrees heat. The bells symbolised the halfway point of our year away. At this precise moment, all the Family Trippers were more than a little homesick. We needed to meet some new friends.

Six months earlier, two families embarked upon a year-long journey around the world. From opposite sides of the Atlantic, one from Washington DC, the other from Scotland. We set off in opposite directions, one family heading east and the other west for a year backpacking around the world. Though we had never met, we had corresponded through our travel blogs and emails. My cunning plan, when I decided to create a website and publish blogs, had worked.

We spent Christmas on opposite sides of Australia but, as fate would have it, we would both be in Sydney at the same time. We hatched a plan to meet on New Year's Day afternoon on the steps of the Sydney Opera House. It felt like a family-based version of that famous railway platform scene in *Brief Encounter*. One family nervously waiting on the steps of the Opera House, the other making their way around the harbour, only knowing what each other looked like from photos, wondering whether we would get on and connect.

It felt like lifelong friends meeting for the first time. Stories of travel, past and future, were traded, the emotions and experience of family travel through the developing and developed world shared. They had been to places we were going and had already visited South America, the final continent of our trip. They told us about the highs and lows, including the time their son nearly drowned in the Galápagos Islands, and its impact on their outlook on travel. We had already visited destinations on their itinerary and were happy to share what we had learnt.

Tips and tricks, lessons and learnings were quickly shared. We regaled each other with the anecdotes which didn't make our blogs, either because you had to be there to get it, or they were the things you wouldn't want your mother to read. The Dads talked about Dad things, like the pressures of continually booking places to stay and the responsibility of trying to get it right, especially when it went wrong. The Mums talked about the challenges of keeping their family safe, clean and well-nourished. The kids played on their phones and Nintendo DS devices.

We understood each other, like only those who had lived such an experience could. The highs and lows, the ifs and maybes, the joy and the anxieties. It felt good to know that all these emotions and experiences weren't just us, they were how people like us should feel. We felt normal again.

We parted company after a couple of hours, heading in separate directions once more. Wiser and more at ease with our identity as a travelling family.

Note to self, if you are going to hire a car from Sydney, do not choose the morning after New Year's Day. You will not be alone. Two frustrating hours of queuing later, we headed through the suburbs and away from Sydney in a southerly direction.

We chatted about how lucky we were to take the kids around the world and how few people are able to have such an experience. But it was a roller coaster, as predicted. We were nearly 200 days in and one in five of those had been all-time greats. Days we will remember for the rest of our lives. Many of the remaining 160 had some great or good moments, and there were very few bad bits.

Occasionally, however, a section of the trip made us think, *Why did we decide to do this?*

We had pre-booked this segment covering the south-east corner of Australia because we realised how busy the school holiday period would be. After Christmas, everyone heads to the beach. So why did we take the 900 kilometres long coast road rather than heading inland through what we later learnt was outstanding scenery? Another tripper lesson learnt. The coastal route was ok, but not the best Australia has to offer.

Looking back at our stunning photos, I realise we were just exhausted and homesick. We simply did not recognise our feelings for what they were.

We also had an inferiority complex. As we arrived at each campsite with our tent, tinpot cooking stove and picnic rug, we gasped with envy at the home from home pitches our Australian neighbours had constructed. Satellite dishes, widescreen TVs, microwaves. Coffee makers, lighting rigs, we even saw one tent contain a washing machine. It was like they had emptied their home for the holidays. And they stayed put. We kept putting that damn tent up and down every other day, sharing the camp kitchen, showers and toilets. Whilst doing it this way made Australia affordable for us, it was hard living on an Asian budget.

We had constructed a ten day route comprising four stops, each about four hours' drive from the other. South Durras near Batemans Bay, Eden, Bairnsdale and Phillip Island. Each stop was remarkably similar. There were stunning sunsets, kangaroos marauding the campsites at night, koalas in trees. We took long walks on beaches, splashed in the surf and enjoyed picnics in forests. We had downtime on the campsite, fun time in the sea, and family time in the car.

There was also the time when Roonagh went to the toilet block in the middle of the night and got locked in the dark. Timer switches on the lights might be environmentally friendly, but they do have drawbacks.

Phillip Island, our final stop, was home to minuscule fairy penguins who emerged from the sea in their hundreds to bed down in their cliffside nests every evening. This sunset extravaganza was not to be missed. We arrived mid-afternoon to ensure we got a great seat. I put my head on a table in the busy café and promptly fell asleep for two hours solid.

When the spectator area opened, we bagged an excellent vantage point in the grandstand. We watched in hushed excitement as the tiny penguins surfed the waves, shook themselves off and waddled up the beach like, well tiny penguins. Both of them. Not hundreds, just two tiny penguins.

This leg of the trip was a chance for some much-needed healthy living. After three months in Asia, Anne and I had both lost weight. I could scarcely afford to do this following my hospitalisation in Sri Lanka two months before the trip. I remember standing at the school gates back in Scotland just a couple of weeks after being in hospital, wearing multiple layers of winter clothes, shivering and chittering as other parents removed their sweaters on a balmy early Spring day.

Our first month in Australia had been a chance to gorge ourselves on wonderful wine, familiar foods and seductive snacks. And then to snack some more as we drove for thousands of kilometres, failing to get sufficient steps most days. The inevitable happened, we went from one extreme to another, the pounds started to pile on, and our livers screamed for mercy. We went dry for this leg of the trip and Anne, a state registered dietitian, made sure the calories came down as well. It was medicine we needed to take. Just in time for one of the highlights of our year and an unexpected one at that.

Melbourne didn't make the original itinerary. It never featured on our radar. What a monumental mistake that would have been. It only made the cut as a place we would fly back to Sydney from. Little did we know we would arrive at an ideal time and fall in love with the place. We booked two nights and ended up staying eight.

Melbourne is cool, funky, modern, cultured, relaxed and extremely sporty. We could not have timed our visit better. Preparations for the Australian Open Tennis, one of the four Grand Slams, were in full swing.

Once we discovered entry to the qualifying tournament was free, we went three times. On our last day in the city, we got tickets for the main show court, the Rod Laver Arena, and watched defending men's champion, Novak Djokovic. Best of all, we watched Rafa Nadal practice in the blistering heat for two hours and managed to get close enough to ask him to autograph our copy of the tournament programme. We may have never been to Wimbledon, but we have been to the Australian Open.

As well as a tour of the 100,000 capacity Melbourne Cricket Ground, the iconic MCG, the boys also attended a one day international cricket match between Australia and South Africa. It was an emotional moment for this anti-apartheid campaigner to see the racially integrated South African team sing their National Anthem *Nkosi Sikelel' iAfrica*. Twenty years on from belting it out as a protest song at Wembley for the prisoner who would later become President.

The weather in Melbourne was extreme. Now I know I am being stereotypical here, we Brits do love to talk about the weather. But this was something else. One day it was 42 degrees hot. At night. We turned up the dial on our hotel air-conditioning, waking every time a power surge disrupted the electricity supply, and then nodding off again once normal service was restored. We heard that some locals spent the entire night trying to cool down on the beach.

The most extreme aspect of this experience was yet to come. The next day the temperature plummeted to a positively chilly 16 degrees centigrade. We were delighted, especially as we were about to spend the day in a car.

The 150 miles long Great Ocean Road is renowned as one of the world's most spectacular driving routes. Built by the military between 1919 and 1932 and dedicated to soldiers killed during World War I, the road is the world's largest war memorial. Having had a break from driving, we hired a car for the day in the middle of our extended Melbourne stay and went for a spin.

Foolishly, I took the long route, so the excursion ended up being ten hours in the car with occasional stops for food or photos. The day's highlight was as advertised, the view of the iconic Twelve Apostles, dramatic limestone rock structures sitting in the crashing waves beyond the white cliff tops.

Somewhat confusingly, there have never been 12 of these dramatic rock stacks, but seven of the original eight remained for our visit. The kids wished that the Apostles had retained one of their previous names, The Sow and Pigs. That would have been much more fun.

Sporting highlights apart, Melbourne may not be a city which presents a long list of must-do attractions. But it had a great vibe and was a terrific place to hang out in the stylish Federation Square, walking or boating along the Yarra River or around the newly developed waterfront where I could not resist embarrassing the kids by posing for a photo with an alluring statue of Kylie Minogue.

We also took the lift to the top of the tallest observation deck in the Southern Hemisphere, the Eureka Tower. The alleged highlight here was a viewing platform known as The Edge, a glass cube bolted onto the side of the 88th floor, leaving visitors suspended almost 300 metres above the city below. I felt sick looking at it then, and ill writing about it now.

Not everyone felt like this though, there was a steady procession of vertigo-defying visitors, including one brave romantic who fell on one knee to propose to his girlfriend, seemingly oblivious to the void below his feet.

Sometimes on this trip, places we thought would be great let us down. There were also real surprises, gems we hadn't expected. For us, Melbourne is one of the best cities in the world, Australia's biggest and best-kept secret. The only disappointment, we didn't squeeze in a visit to Ramsay Street, home of TV soap *Neighbour*s.

Sydney

"Aussie Aussie Aussie Oi Oi Oi."

This boisterous refrain rang around the streets of Sydney's City Business District.

Australia Day, 26th January. Marking the anniversary of the arrival of British convict ships in 1788 and the colonisation of this continent by a small distant island.

Australia Day, a day of culture and celebration. Or a day off work to let one's hair down in the middle of summer with a few tinnies? To party like it's 1788.

For the indigenous Aboriginal population, the day is reviled as *Invasion Day*. Despite a recent Prime Ministerial apology to the aboriginal people for all past misdemeanours, breakfast TV and newspapers were still full of debate and opinion about whether the day should be moved, amended or scrapped altogether.

Either way, the authorities were committed to persuading the locals to come out and celebrate in Sydney. There were events across the city and TV adverts berating those who preferred to stay at home.

It was not just the kids who were attending class at the World School. We all were. Having been educated in the UK, we had a British and European perspective on history. When I studied History at school, the syllabus finished in 1815 with the Battle of Waterloo. Our teachers never explored the full impact of empire, the slave trade and the many injustices inflicted on civilizations around the world.

I could now see the colonial legacy playing out in front of our eyes around the world. Now I was in a proper History lesson.

We spent more than half our year in the Southern Hemisphere, much of it around the Pacific Rim. World maps looked different here. Britain looked smaller and less significant. We started to understand colonial, military and contemporary history from a different perspective.

We were the invaders, not the rulers. The aggressors, not explorers nor peacemakers as I had been taught at school. It turned out the kids weren't the only ones getting an improved education as we travelled around the world. Explaining these new concepts to our young children was not easy, but we made sure they were exposed to cultural experiences wherever we went, whether through dance, sport or boomerang throwing.

For the first time in 100 years, Australia Day coincided with the Chinese New Year. Darling Harbour, down at the waterfront and bordering Chinatown, was the place to watch the festivities. Overnight, the weather turned from 40 degrees heat into a typical dreich Scottish day. If there were fireworks, we never saw them. It was the equivalent of looking for a black cat in a dark room, with the lights off and your eyes shut. But the people watching was interesting and the beer tasted good. Even if, as the evening progressed, the men did chunder.

Queensland
Water, water everywhere

The following morning, we picked up a camper van for a month-long journey from Sydney to Cairns and the tropical north.

This leg of the trip had been cemented in the budget from an early stage. Even though we had known it would stretch our finances, it was something we were eager to experience.

Upgrading from a tent to a camper van was something we had to do to experience the quintessential Aussie road trip. We loved the upgrade in home comforts. The kids watched a series of DVDs on Australian wildlife, an advance on games of Uno. The onboard toilet was a marked improvement on midnight treks across campsites. It felt luxurious to pull into the side of the road in a toilet emergency and obtain instant relief. Even if I did occasionally forget to empty the sluice tank in time before it overflowed.

Having a fridge expanded the range of culinary delights we could all enjoy, providing some temporary relief from our staple meal, pasta with tomato sauce. Sat up high in the driver's seat, with the kids happy in the back, we felt like kings of the road.

Looking at the map, the most exciting activities and areas appeared to be north of Brisbane, some 564 miles north of Sydney. For the first two days, we just kept driving. We had an eagle eye on the weather forecast. It looked stormy up north and there were reports of road closures. Bypassing the Gold and Sunshine Coasts, we kept going, motivated by promises of exotic treasures to come.

Mon Repos, on the Queensland coast near Bundaberg, roughly halfway between Sydney and Cairns, supports the largest concentration of nesting marine turtles on the eastern Australian mainland. It has the most significant loggerhead turtle nesting population in the South Pacific. It is unique, as it is a nesting ground for three of the world's seven remaining turtle species: loggerhead, green and flatback. All of which are seriously endangered.

These incredible creatures date back to the time when dinosaurs roamed the earth. They survived the Ice Age unscathed, turtles not dinosaurs that is, and genetically speaking are almost unchanged. Remarkably our knowledge of them is scant and the work done by Queensland Environmental Protection Agency in carrying out research, conservation and education is commendable. It is also crucial for the turtles' survival.

We were lucky to witness, under a star-filled Southern Hemisphere night sky, 130 baby turtles emerging from the sand at the start of their lives. Well, I say the start of their lives. They had already been alive for five days, buried in the sand, slowly making their way to the surface, and surviving off the yolk of the egg they had just escaped from. And then they popped up onto the beach in one great heap, like popcorn exploding in a pan.

They slowly made their way to a holding pen where a ranger explained that only one in 1,000 make it to adulthood. This batch were all females; the sex of turtles is determined by the sand's temperature where the eggs incubate. One consequence of rising global temperatures could result in the removal of the male half of the species, leading directly to their extinction. This on top of the perils of the sea, namely predators and human pollution. Just like dolphins, many turtles choke to death on human detritus such as plastic bags and fishing lines or are maimed by marine craft. Depressing stuff.

Anyway, the wee lassies were then released to make their journey to the sea. We all formed a tunnel of light with our torches, stood in a row with our legs apart, and the baby turtles made a run for it. When they hit the waves, they were knocked back and crawled over our feet, ready to have another go. Roonagh thought this was just the cutest thing ever.

On their way into the sea, a genetic imprint is made which tells the females where they are so when, or should I say if, they reach maturity they can come back to lay their eggs. They will return, not necessarily to the same beach as is commonly thought, but to the same area. Male turtles never return to land, they have a cushy life of eating, mating and trying to stay alive. Those turtles that manage to avoid all these challenges can survive up to 80 years old.

Next up, we had an unexpected treat. A female adult turtle dragged herself up the beach to lay a clutch of eggs. Quite a sight. She dug a hole about 60 centimetres deep and then, over the next 15 minutes, started to lay hundreds of ping-pong ball sized eggs. She then undertook the exhausting task of re-filling the hole to ensure predatory scavengers such as dingo wouldn't be able to find the eggs. The process took another half hour, with many rests between the countless strokes of her flippers.

Sitting next to this remarkable beast, watching her do what nature has created her for, was a humbling sight. This was her only duty as a mother, when she makes it back to sea that is the end of her role. No dirty nappies, no sleepless nights, no unruly teenagers. No maternal bond, no birthday parties, no family trips. No reward, other than doing what comes naturally and doing her bit to maintain the species' survival.

A quarter of a century before the day we swam on the Great Barrier Reef, I travelled to Wembley Stadium to support my hometown football team, Boston United, in a cup final. We had a terrific day even though we lost the match. The next day I turned on the news to see the horrors of the Bradford football stadium fire, which killed dozens of supporters.

Twenty-five years later, and on the other side of the world, we woke up tired but content after a memorable day on the Great Barrier Reef, to learn about the devastating bushfires down in Victoria. 173 people lost their lives, at that time the worst loss of life from any recorded Australian bushfire. We had driven through some of the areas now reduced to ash just a couple of weeks previously. Flags were at half-mast in Queensland and it brought home to us the strength of the power of nature. Killer fires in the South and deadly floods in the North.

Our trip to Fitzroy Reef Lagoon provided an opportunity to witness the glory, rather than the terror, of nature and to reflect on humanity's capacity to damage our inheritance.

The Great Barrier Reef is 2,000 kilometres in length, stretching from Southern Queensland to Papua New Guinea. A living organism, it continually changes and evolves. Some coral grows 12 inches in a year, others one millimetre. A human footprint can last for years, killing the coral it touches.

Snorkelling through the coral, carefully ensuring I never touched it, was one of those trip highlights I will always remember. Even if I did forget to sun cream the back of my thighs, exposed where the water pushed up my swimming shorts, and my sunburn lasted for the best part of five months. Driving the camper van was nothing short of excruciating for the next few days.

Roonagh wrote

First we got a pick up from the campsite. We went on a big red boat. First we went on the bumpy 1 1/2 hour journey to Fitzroy lagoon. We got morning tea then we went on the glass bottom boat. We saw lots of coral and fish. We saw a piece of coral that was 26,000 years old! Then we got a swim (snorkel) in the sea. After that we got the reef teach while we had lunch.

We learnt that coral can heal bones and can be used as a fake eye. Fish cannot see blue. Then we went on the glass bottom boat for the second time, coral's closest relative is the jellyfish. We saw fire coral and brain coral and lots of other corals that I didn't know the name of. We saw Stingray but no turtles. Then we got in the sea and snorkelled over the reef after that lots of people jumped off the boat including that. Finally we went on the boat back to the campsite. We had chips and salad for tea."

Rory's account was:

We had to wake up early. Then we got picked up for sickening 2 hour journey to Fitzroy reef lagoon The Great Barrier reef. As we arrived at this piece of paradise we encountered a green turtle that really rose our expectations. First we all went on the glass bottom boat. On the glass bottom boat Isaac showed us a piece of coral that was 26,000 years old and it is lucky if it even grows a millimetre a year. Whereas you get stags that can grow up to two inches a year.

Then we learnt that the sea isn't blue, it is just the way our eyes are because the herbivore fish don't see blue but they are usually blue. The predators see what we see, blue, and if the fish is blue the predator won't be able to see the fish. After the glass bottom boat we listened to reef teach while we had our lunch. At reef teach we learnt that coral is great for medication because you can now get a coral eyeball and coral can fix a bird's wing in two weeks. Corel's closest relative is the jellyfish, for coral is like an upside down motionless jellyfish.

Then we went on the glass bottom boat again and dad got off and snorkelled 800 metres back to the seaquest. The three of us stayed on the boat and we saw two blue ringed stingray. Then we swam and saw the Great Barrier reef at its best. Then we tried out the glass bottom kayaks. Then we sailed back to the Town of 1770. For tea we had salad.

The kids' description of this amazing day beautifully captured our experience. Vivid colours, the heat of the summer sun, the glory of nature at its finest made this another of the top ten days of the trip.

Eventually, we had to accept the inevitable. There was no way we would be able to drive to Northern Queensland. Following two cyclones and the heaviest monsoonal rains in 30 years, 60% of the State was under floodwater and had been declared a disaster zone. Ironically 54% of the land was also officially in drought. I am not sure how that maths works, but that is what we read.

The main road to Cairns was closed in several places and many towns were cut off. One area had been isolated for four weeks and was at risk of remaining so for another six. The locals were reportedly alarmed at the low beer stocks.

The floods washed crocodiles and snakes out of rivers. In Townsville, further up on our route, a guy ran over a crocodile in his car. Both survived. There were stories of dogs going missing.

Another cyclone was anticipated in the next few days.

We reluctantly decided we had no choice but to turn around and take a leisurely route back to Brisbane. We could stop at some of the places we had bombed past on the way up and chill out a bit. Tropical Queensland could be saved for another time as unfinished business. Better safe than sorry. At least we weren't trying to go to work or school in the snow and ice back home.

The Gold Coast seemed to be more suited for young backpackers and holidaymaking couples than travelling families, so we headed to the Sunshine Coast for a delightful week of picnics, ice creams and bodyboarding.

The South Pacific Ocean waters were so warm they felt like a heated swimming pool. We splashed around for hours and rode those waves like professionals. One of those two statements is true. Before the trip, the kids and I used to head down to our local beach sporting our wet suits. Australia put paid to that. When you have ridden waves in warm bath-like water, it is less enjoyable to shiver, fully suited, in the freezing cold waters of the North Sea. It never felt like fun again. I can't think why.

It was a week when little happened, and yet remains one of my favourite times on the trip. Fate had seemingly conspired against us, robbing us of the opportunity to visit the Tropical North. Yet, here was what we had been chasing all along, the reason we were doing this entire experience. Not to see amazing places, not to tick off items on a bucket list. It was a leaky bucket that always seemed to have new destinations added into it, no matter how many incredible and iconic places we visited. No, we were just laughing, relaxing and being a family. It's the interruptions along the way which make the journey worthwhile.

Here in Australia, just as back home in Scotland, the children had gone back to school. The working year was in full swing as businesses and employees struggled to stay afloat in the eye of the storm of a recession. And we were just having fun. As a family. Husband and wife. Parent and child. Brother and sister. On the other side of the world, we found ourselves in the waves.

We are not big fans of zoos. As the trip progressed, our uneasiness grew. The zoo in Kobe, where we finally saw Pandas and several distressed big cats, underlined this belief. Conservation is critical, and many zoos play a crucial role, but too many are exploitative with questionable animal welfare records. To be fair, the best zoos play an important educational role, especially for those who never have our good fortune to see so many exotic species in their natural environment.

Looking back, I don't know if we let ourselves down or just decided the kids needed to see those unique Australian animals we had not seen in the wild. Either way, we found ourselves with two excited kids in the queue for the Lone Pine Koala Sanctuary one sunny Brisbane morning. The kids were delighted, and this showed in Rory's daily diary:

It was a bit like a zoo but the purpose was to see the Aussie wildlife we've missed out on. First we went to the wombats. There are three types of wombat two of which we saw, the southern hairy nosed wombat and the common wombat.

The third of these three species is the northern hairy nosed wombat which is possibly one of the most endangered animals in the world. All 120 of them live in the same place in Queensland and no researchers or other human beings are allowed in the area apart from the Rangers. The wombats were about the size of a small pig and were very dozy but they can run up to 40 kilometres per hour and could easily push a door down.

Then we went and fed the Kangaroos and wallabies. There was one wallaby I just adored. It was so delicate and fragile.

We also saw the big Reds. The way the Roos licked you when you fed them was slightly strange. Then we watched the koala talk but we didn't learn anything, but I don't suppose we learnt anything from the wombat talk either. Before we left, we went to see the Dingoes and Tasmanian Devils.

In the blink of an eye, our Australian summer finished at the end of February. We travelled many thousands of miles, stayed in iconic cities, and witnessed the extraordinary diversity of life on our planet. We experienced culture which we had naively expected to be much like ours back home, but was different in many ways:

> Rules Rules Rules- regulations in campsites went on forever.

> Shop assistants who spoke to us the moment we walked in a store and kept on talking to us.

> Bottle stores, a separate place from the supermarket where we purchased alcohol, and left shame-faced with it in a brown paper bag.

> Look, responses prefaced with "*look,*" which initially sounded rude to our ears but was just a local idiom.

> Portion control, Anne having to almost beg a chip shop owner to let her have a $5 bag of chips- "look, there are only four of you, you can't possibly eat that many chips." We did. We come from Scotland.

We ended our three months down under back in Sydney. 1,500 photos later. Overall, we had a fantastic time. As they say Down Under, "it was all good." It was relatively tame compared to our African and Asian adventures, but we experienced so much quality family time. But we weren't done yet.

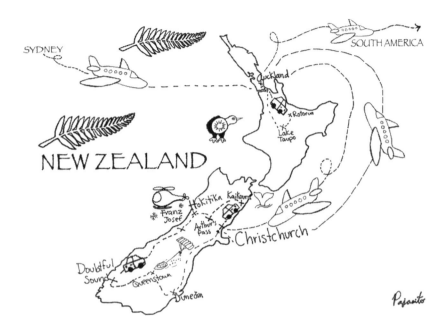

SYDNEY

SOUTH AMERICA

Auckland

×Rotorua

Lake
Taupo

NEW ZEALAND

Hokitika Kaikoura

Franz
Josef

Arthur's
Pass

Christchurch

Doubtful
Sound

Queenstown

Dunedin

Pajarito

New Zealand
Sulphur, speedboats and sea lions

New Zealand's Border Force takes great care to ensure no alien species can enter the country. Fortunately, Brits are allowed. But the entry procedure was rigorous in the extreme. No dirt or soil is allowed on shoes, boots or tents. That way, foreign nasties can't get into the country's ecosystem and cause untold damage to flora and fauna.

We had, of course, pre-booked a taxi to take us into the city for our first night's stay. Coming from high-rise Sydney and Melbourne, it was surprising to drive past one and two storey homes with massive gardens. Auckland seemed to go on for miles. Apart from a few sky-scraping hotels and office blocks in the compact centre, the city was very low-rise. The highlight was the 328 metres tall Sky Tower, seen worldwide every New Year's Eve on television sets, when the first major city in the world enters the New Year, and celebrates with a flourish of fireworks. There was no such drama on our visit, other than crazy people walking around the high open ledge and then jumping off the top. For the avoidance of doubt, they were not suicidal, just committed and enthusiastic sky jumpers.

Auckland was a very nautical place. Spreading out from the main harbour and along the coast, was a series of marinas, packed with yachts and pleasure cruisers to keep the locals busy at weekends. There was also a massive commercial port crammed with cranes, containers and captains skilfully navigating gigantic ships.

The day after our arrival, we took a local train to stay in the suburbs with one of Anne's work colleagues who was enjoying a two year sabbatical in Auckland. Stepping onto the train felt like walking into the United Nations. I don't think we had ever seen such a melting pot of races, colours and backgrounds in one place before.

New Zealand has a diverse population. Two-thirds are of European heritage, 16% are indigenous Maori, with the remaining 20% originating predominately from Asia and the South Pacific Islands.

As we travelled around the country, we learnt that just as with the Aboriginal population in Australia, and the Native American peoples in the United States, the Maori are socially and economically disadvantaged, leading to unemployment, crime, drugs, homelessness and deprivation. Things are not always as happy under the surface as they first appear to the casual tourist.

Just like Sydney, Auckland was strangely familiar. It felt like a piece of Europe cast apart. We knew we were on the other side of the world because Rory and I watched televised football matches in our pyjamas with breakfast cereal on our knees.

We were eight months in, and as lovely as it was to stay with friends for a short while, we were becoming tired of the constant moving. We started to feel we repeatedly saw different versions of the same thing. Just another jungle, forest or beach. African people, Asian people, Australian people.

They have a saying in Thailand, "Same Same but Different." The world was starting to feel a bit repetitive and we missed carpet. That might sound silly, but we had a beautiful home back in Scotland. Five bedrooms, all with carpet. Two lounges, both with carpet. And five bathrooms, admittedly with no carpet. How we missed those soft fibres cushioning every footstep, unlike the unwelcoming tiled and wooden floors with which we were now familiar. Of course, it wasn't actually carpet we missed, it was our home and all its comforts.

"I don't know about you, but I am tired of continually moving. Do you think we should just do these three weeks in New Zealand, scrap South America and go home?"

Our plan at this point was to spend three weeks in New Zealand, followed by four months in South America.

I looked at Anne amazed. "Are you mad? I know exactly what you mean, but our home is rented out, we would have nowhere to live."

In the end, we doubled our time in New Zealand, equally spent between the two main islands, North and South, and reduced the South American leg of our travels to three months.

As we started to settle into our latest destination, New Zealand reignited our travel flame. We were bitten by the bug again. Our Va Va Voom was back. Alongside Japan and Madagascar, New Zealand became our favourite country of the trip. A real home from home. Unlike our campsite life in

Australia, or the *West Island* as they call it in New Zealand, we stayed in some great apartments and motels which fitted our budget. The improvement in our living conditions and the glorious autumn weather doubtless influenced our sense of wellbeing.

Then there was the landscape. Unique, breath-taking and varied. Simply wonderful. The South Island is incredible, so majestic. Sandy beaches stretch on forever, forests verdant with giant trees and massive ferns. Glaciers, mountains, thermal springs, mud pools and icy fjords carved into the coastline like the veins on the fern leaf, the country's national symbol. Even if New Zealand were only the North Island, it would still be a stunning location. Put the two together and bingo, you have a drive-in movie set. *Lord of the Rings* proves why these locations are so prized. As are Scotland's, albeit the volcanoes here are more alive and dangerous than ours. You wouldn't build Edinburgh Castle on a New Zealand volcano.

New Zealand felt a little like a version of Scotland on the other side of the world. There are strong links between the two countries, and we felt at home. The pace of life, however, felt slower, sometimes decades slower. And that is not meant in any way as a criticism, more a compliment.

As we travelled around the globe, the kids learnt so much. They were able to compare and contrast subjects in different countries. Especially natural history. The planet, its plants, animals and birds. The impact of the world's fast-changing climate became an easy conversation starter everywhere we went. Taxi drivers were often interested in finding out whether the effects of global warming, as it was called in 2008, were just affecting their country, or had we seen them elsewhere.

We were fascinated by a word we kept seeing in the Southern Hemisphere, *Gondwana*. It popped up so many times. 130 million years ago the continental plates shifted, various parts broke apart, and a new supercontinent was formed. Gondwana later split to form Africa and Asia and created new landmasses we visited such as Madagascar, Australia and New Zealand. The latter was the most recent to form, emerging from the sea many millions of years later.

Some of the animals which evolved from Gondwana are obviously related. For example, the lemurs of Madagascar and the possums of Australia. Extinct birds such as the Moa of New Zealand and the Elephant Bird of Madagascar, are related to the Ostrich of South Africa and the Emu and Southern Cassowary of Australia. Some are less obvious to connect, such as the furry rodent-like Rock Dassie of Table Mountain, closely related to the Elephant. I have no idea how that works.

The evolution of the planet itself also fascinated the kids. For example, volcanology, not a topic which would have grabbed my attention at school. They learnt about the inner core, outer core, mantle and crust of the earth and saw the impact of seismic shifts below the surface, from Japan to New Zealand. We even had our schedule changed by the tragic events of the Chengdu earthquake in China just before we left Scotland.

On our final day in Auckland, before we caught a flight to the South Island, we climbed the largest of the 50 volcanoes in the Auckland area. Rangitoto is the most recently created volcanic island in New Zealand. Formed 600 years ago, it emerged from the sea in a massive explosion of steam, fire and magma, viewed from neighbouring islands by the presumably terrified Maori population. We walked enthralled through lava caves and climbed up its forested slopes. I explained to the kids that, in evolutionary timescales, we were just a few seconds on from the volcanic eruption that gave birth to the island.

Gondwana lives, and so did *Tripper Spirit*.

This really happened.

Auckland Airport, just before security in the Domestic Departures Lounge.

The lady at the Sumo Salads Bar says to me, "Is that your egg and bacon butty?"

"No" says I, "It's not mine."

"It's mine" says Neil Finn, lead singer of Crowded House.

I had always wanted to visit Christchurch on the South Island. My Godmother moved there when I was in my teens. She married and settled down. I always thought that I would head out and visit her at some point. Sadly, her husband passed away after a few years, and she moved back home to Grimsby. I am sure Grimsby is lovely, but it never had the same appeal.

We checked into the sumptuous Heritage Hotel in Christchurch, situated in the grand Old Government Buildings on Cathedral Square, for my latest 34th birthday. Before the trip, I decided that whenever I was asked my age, I would say, "34 and a bit." It always made me feel good about myself, especially as I was now entering my 43rd year.

Christchurch has a reputation for being the most English place in New Zealand, but that was not our experience. It was cosmopolitan, with a balanced mix of locals, travellers and charming cafés. We even had an evening meal in one of them. It was my birthday, after all. We appreciate our time in

Christchurch even more now, it suffered so much devastation in a massive earthquake two years later.

One of the trip's rules was that we made birthdays special, given we couldn't splash out on many presents because we would have had to carry them around with us. The birthday boy or girl had the privilege of choosing somewhere special to stay and the family's activity for the day. I was getting old so fancied a pipe and slippers day, including stretching out on the sofa and watching my team Manchester United thump Newcastle United 2-1 in the league. A rare treat indeed. Not the result (sorry Geordie friends) but sitting on a sofa with a beer or two watching football.

Our route around the South Island was planned by the kids. It was time for a geography lesson. We purchased a large, illustrated guide to the South Island and gave them the freedom to plan our itinerary. They loved this activity which helped pass many hours in the car and led to us visiting some fantastic places we might otherwise not have experienced.

We had unfinished business with whales. On too many occasions, we arrived in new destinations to be told there were usually whales just off the coast, yet we always turned up at the wrong time of year. Or if we were in the right place at the right time, the cost was prohibitive. The only occasion we had headed out to sea searching for whales in South Africa had resulted in no viewings and a bruised kidney.

Unfortunately, we figured it would be the wrong time of year to see them in New Zealand. On this basis, we excluded the South Island's premier whale watching destination, Kaikoura, from our schedule. I had done my research, or so I thought. Fortunately, the Tourist Information Office in Christchurch was better informed than me. It turned out that Kaikoura had a resident pod of sperm whales and more dolphins than you can shake a stick at or steer a fleet of tourist boats towards.

We immediately re-jigged our plans and headed two hours up the east coast of the South Island. We tried not to worry about the adverse weather forecast we had just watched on TV. But of course, we were concerned given our track record. Was the South African episode about to repeat itself?

We need not have been anxious as we were about to have another of those amazing days.

Roonagh continues the story:

Phew! It's a great day for whale watching because that's what we're doing today! We got straight to the ticket office and got a bus to the boat. Our first sighting was ABSOLUTELY AMAZING, it was five sperm whales. We saw two whales doing deep water feeding (slapping their tales against the water).

We travelled a little more and there right in front of us were 200-400 Dusky Dolphins, the Acrobats of the Sea. They were doing back flips, jumps, leaps and all sorts of things! They were beautiful and definitely the best dolphin sighting I have EVER seen! Unfortunately we have to leave the Dolphins but we got to see another sperm whale.

For our last sighting we saw a seal colony sunbathing on the rocks. We were VERY lucky for what we saw and got some great photos.

Six sperm whales, over 200 acrobatic dolphins and a colony of fur seals were a fantastic sight to behold. We didn't have time, but it was also possible to swim with seals and dolphins.

Kaikoura delivered for us. Our advice to other travellers is don't bother elsewhere, save your money for Kaikoura, New Zealand. It is all here in one place. Truly special.

Here's what Rory made of it:

One thing we still haven't accomplished yet on this trip is the sighting of the King of the Sea, the whale. We have been unlucky given we have been on lots of boats out to sea. Hopefully we will be fortunate enough to see the sperm whale, the largest toothed whale, at the Kaikoura Canyon, a bit like McDonald's for teenage whales. I wasn't hopeful even though the 9:00 o'clock boats yesterday saw three sperm whales and 200 dusky Dolphins. I just hope 150 pounds doesn't go down the drain again like our unsuccessful well watching trip in South Africa but this time we are in the whale watching capital of New Zealand Kaikoura.

So we went to the whale watching centre and got a bus to Paikea (whale rider) our boat. We have to sit in the main cabin inside while we were going out to see. But we didn't go right out because we could still see the mountains, in fact we were probably only just past the continental shelf but that was as far as we needed to go to see a whale.

Oh, if I say we were hoping to see a whale well we've seen 5 already! Everyone suddenly jumped up from their seats and run up the stairs to the upper deck. They stayed on the surface for five or 10 minutes and one by one went with the flick of the tail to swim and dive at the Kaikoura Canyon for 45 minutes to one hour.

Then we were told by radio from another boat that there was a pod of dusky dolphin the acrobats of the sea and there wasn't just a few there were three or 400 of them we were in for a treat! As we approached them we learnt why they are and always will be the acrobats of the sea. The flips and leaps they did were just out of this world absolutely amazing. If you thought one of doing this is super then try seeing 400 or so! Then we saw a solitary sperm whale but he only stayed on the surface for no time at all. To round up a great morning we said hello to some New Zealand fur seals on the way back.

When we set out on this journey, one of our objectives was to see the world through the children's eyes, and days like this made it worthwhile. As parents, we loved it when our kids had the privilege of incredible interactions with nature and admired how they expressed themselves in their diaries. It was one terrific English lesson. There was no doubt their writing styles were coming on leaps and bounds. Just like the dolphins.

Arthur's Pass cuts through the Southern Alps to the West Coast. We stayed on a sheep station just before Arthurs Pass Mountain Park, a cool little place appropriately called Flock Hill. Having survived tents and van-life in Australia, we loved the relative luxury of a three-bed wooden chalet with a kitchen and bathroom for about half what the camper van cost us. We were like Heidi if she had won the lottery. Three bedrooms, SKY TV, decking and fabulous mountain views.

We were gutted to only stay for one night. Even more so when we got to our next stop at the grey seaside town of Hokitika. Our residence was a garden shed on a (should be) condemned campsite behind the Dairy Factory. If I had known what I had booked, I wouldn't have bothered. Another excellent example of how much better any trip would be with the benefit of hindsight. But where's the fun in that?

One thing that makes the South Island's coastline so spectacular is the expansive driftwood piled on its black sand beaches. Great for imaginative play and creative photography. We spent many happy hours building pirate ships out of wood and taking arty photos of our creations. Then there was the surf. Unlike Queensland's beaches, where you can walk out way into the sea, here the surf rises to two or three metres before crashing tumultuously onto the shore. It felt like we could hear it echoing miles away.

As we drove down the coast, the weather deteriorated. Undeterred, we had a lovely walk to the top of stunningly high waterfalls set amid forests, water dripping off bright-green leaves and giant ferns. We had great fun watching colourful and ravenous mountain parrots destroy the seat of some poor punter's mountain bike. Called Kea, these indigenous birds clearly had a healthy appetite.

In Auckland, Rory had picked up a novel about these feisty creatures, a Kiwi version of *Watership Down* if you will, which he read in Ecuador when he was under the weather. *Beak of the Moon* remains his favourite childhood book. He has two copies just in case, another example of how the World Classroom kept on giving.

This area should be an unmissable part of anyone's itinerary. As should a walk around Lake Matheson with fabulous views of the icy landscape. Unfortunately, Mount Cook was hiding in the clouds, so we didn't see mountain reflections in the glacial lake, but it was still spectacular. Even if an annoying English person did her best to spoil it by droning on about economic doom and gloom back home. *Shut up, you're so annoying, we're on our trip and in denial, ok*, we thought inwardly. Being British, we wouldn't say such a thing in front of her.

Five days after my birthday, it was Roonagh's turn. It is always an expensive week in our family, as it was for my parents, my sister's birthday falling the day after mine. Every year.

Back home, it usually rains on Roonagh's birthday. She had decided she would like to have a helicopter ride for her treat. I guess it was cheaper than buying her a pony.

The plan was to fly over Franz Josef Glacier in a helicopter on the morning of her birthday. True to form, it rained all day, and the trip was cancelled. But we did go the following morning, technically still her birthday given we were 13 hours ahead of the UK. We woke to bright blue skies and excited children. One quick phone call and it was "Come on kids, get ready, we're going up." We were in the air by 9:30 am. Or, with the time difference, 8:30 pm on Roonagh's ninth birthday.

Franz and Fox are two of many glaciers in New Zealand, but two of only three in the world which descend into rainforest. A result of westerly winds dumping buckets of rain and moisture on the mountain slopes. In case you are wondering, the other rainforest-based glacier is in Argentina.

A glacier is essentially a river of ice descending down a mountain, through a valley forged by its own weight. When snow falls on the top of the mountain, it compresses the snow underneath. This in turn creates pressure on the glacier, slowly moving the whole mass downwards. The snow we saw fall that morning would take five years to make its way to the bottom of the glacier.

It was our first time in a helicopter, another bucket list tick and a new mode of transport for the family. The views were, of course, spectacular. Why wouldn't they be? The whole landscape was laid out before our eyes: mountains, lakes and rainforest. Then there were the glaciers themselves, sparkling like fields of diamonds beneath us. We went right up Franz and down Fox, before sweeping over the plain back to base. The whole thing lasted 30 minutes and felt like about five, always a sign of a good experience. The highlight was undoubtedly the ten minute stop on top of the ice. After a few photos, it was time for a snowball fight. According to Rory's diary, "*Competitive Dad*" won. We celebrated Roonagh's birthday treat later that day with hot chocolate and marshmallows.

The undulating drive from Franz Josef to Lake Wanaka through rainforest, ocean panoramas, the spectacular Haast valley and the Mount Aspiring (to what?) Mountains must be one of the world's great drives. We saw seals on the beach, thundering waterfalls, blue water tumbling over huge boulders, superb mountain vistas and yes, quite a few sheep. After an overnight stop at Lake Wanaka, Roonagh and I went cycling on the lake in a huge water-bike contraption like something out of *It's a Knockout*. We then headed an hour further south to THE place to jump off bridges with a long rope attached to your feet, Queenstown.

We didn't bungee. We're not that kind of family, and it was never going to be an option for *vertigo man*. On top of that, Anne suffers from motion sickness, usually brought on by my driving, but on the trip by choppy boat rides and crazy drivers.

However, it would be mad to come to beautiful Queenstown, the Southern Hemisphere's adventure capital and not push ourselves a bit.

There was no shortage of activity choice in and around Queenstown, from skydiving to zip wires. Worryingly for me, most of the exertions seemed to involve the sky, or jumping off things. Roonagh and I were the more naturally inclined adrenaline junkies, having wetted our whistles with zorbing in Thailand. Which basically meant being strapped above each other inside a large, inflated bubble and rolling down a hillside. We laughed, screamed, laughed and laughed some more.

Emboldened by that experience, we decided to have a go at parasailing. We looked at tiny figures parasailing over water in many places and thought, *Crikey, we could never do that*. But we had a closer look and figured it was JUST within our limits. It did indeed prove to be so, at least while we were living off *Tripper Spirit*.

Tentatively stepping onto a speed boat, with the aptly named Remarkable Mountains looking down on us, we headed out onto the shimmering waters of Lake Wakatipu and waited our turn. Fortunately, we were able to get tandem flights so the kids could take turns to look after their nervous parents.

Parasailing is quite simple. You step into a harness resembling a baby bouncer hanging off a door, and then you are attached to a rope. The winch then slowly turns, and as the boat goes forward, you go up. And up. The ascent was smooth, the views were tremendous, and our nerves quickly dissipated. Actually, the views were "*Remarkable*." Queenstown must be one of the best places in the world to parasail. After 12 glorious minutes, we were hauled back down and planted our feet on the boat below.

Another adrenaline-inducing activity had taken place the preceding day. This time only father and daughter participated. We went jet boating in Skippers Canyon on the Shotover River. The bus journey to Skippers Canyon was an adventure sport in itself. Forty-five minutes on a narrow gravel road perched precariously, with a 100 metres drop to the valley below. Several times we thought we weren't going to make it.

We made it to the river, and then it was time to be driven nearly straight at a rock. We were soon screaming and laughing with delight as we sped along at speeds up to 85 kilometres per hour, bumping off the four inch deep riverbed, narrowly avoiding boulders and cliff faces. The highlights were the saturating and exhilarating 360-degree spins. It was fun but scary. I don't know if I wet myself in the excitement, but even if I did, no-one would have ever noticed.

We visited the original bungee bridge, too small for modern-day jumpers but way high enough for us. We plucked up courage and walked across but didn't jump. No chance. According to Billy Connolly, you can bungee for free in Queenstown, but only if you are naked. Billy being Billy, that is precisely what he did.

Queenstown was one of those places we loved being with the kids. But we also wondered what it would be like after dark when the older young people came out to play. They partied hard given the state of the streets at 9:00 am, or as we knew it, mid-morning. Fun was to be had on these streets. Sadly, we were always tucked up in bed with the wee ones. Sometimes we felt we would return and do much of the trip again without the kids, just to see what these places would be like in the dark. Who knows, maybe we will return one day, although I suspect we will be too old for partying by that point.

Having learnt all about glaciers, it was now time to spend a night on a fjord. Not a misspelling of a motor car, a fjord is what's left when a glacier has left the building, leaving a valley which is then flooded by the sea. A kind of upside-down glacier if you like.

The best-known fjord in New Zealand is Milford Sound which receives 5,000 visitors a day, advancing with military-style precision in a convoy of boats and a squadron of helicopters and planes. We opted for its more tranquil and lesser-known cousin, Doubtful Sound, the second largest of New Zealand's 14 fjords. Three times longer than its more illustrious neighbour, Doubtful has a sea surface roughly ten times larger and a depth of up to 430 metres.

This area of New Zealand, known as *Fjordland*, is home to a stunning array of marine mammals. As well as an encounter with a colony of fur seals, we had an incredible dolphin experience, a pod of Bottlenose dolphins bow-riding with our boat for what felt like an eternity. We had heard about this dolphin behaviour before but never had the good fortune to experience it. The speed these amazing creatures maintain is breath-taking, and to see them surfing waves and leaping through the air is a sight to behold.

Captain James Cook popped up everywhere on our antipodean adventure, including in the Town of 1770 where we had been based for our trip to the Great Barrier Reef. Guess what happened in the Town of 1770? Yes, well done, Captain Cook landed there in 1770.

Cook is also credited with giving Doubtful Sound its name, albeit by making a bit of a cockup. As he passed along the Tasman Sea charting the coast of New Zealand, he saw the entrance to the Sound and said something like, "I doubt we'll be able to get up there chaps" and scribbled "*Doubtful Harbour*" on his chart. Off he headed up the coast, looking for the next best thing, leaving this beautiful fjord undisturbed for another couple of decades. The Sound was discovered 23 years later in 1793 by Spanish explorers.

We opted to splash out (no dreadful pun intended) on an overnight cruise. After a one hour ride across beautiful Lake Manapouri, and a 40 minute coach transfer through the mountainous rainforest of the Wilmot Pass, we boarded the Fjordland Navigator, our home for the next 20 hours.

The passengers were a motley crew, a combination of weary backpackers holed up in quad rooms and *silver surfers* in the posh seats. We were the former. The great news was that there was an all you can eat buffet. We feasted till we could feast no more. Belatedly, we had that Christmas feeling, full for two days and digesting for four.

The crew were uber-friendly, not in a taxi way, and the skipper was more than happy to have the kids at the wheel whenever they wished. Roonagh and I took kayaks out at sunset, as the glacial walls were mirrored on the burnt orange still waters. The following morning, we stood on the blustery deck, coffee and doughnuts in hand, watching dolphins swim and pirouette in our wake.

Doubtful Sound is a photographer's dream. Not just for the wildlife and stunning scenery, but especially for the reflections of the valley on the water. Really dreamy. Will we see better water anywhere else? Apart from Scotland of course.

We were a long way from home, geographically speaking. We couldn't have been much further away, on the other side of the world, with 13 hours' time difference. In effect a day ahead. It was Autumn, yet Spring at home. But when we travelled down to Dunedin, we felt like we were back in Scotland. Mostly anyway.

For starters, the weather was just like home. Wet, cold and windy. Just the way we are supposed to like it and pretend we do. The wind may have been blowing off the South Pacific Ocean, but the way it howled it could easily have been the North Sea.

Secondly, the street names. Dunedin is renowned for being a slice of Scotland in New Zealand. In the 1860s, early settlers gave Dunedin its name, *Dunedin* being the Gaelic name for New Edinburgh. The city planners decided to lay the city out with Edinburgh's street names. It felt strange cruising along Princes Street, then heading down Leith Walk and on to Musselburgh. Places sounded right but looked wrong.

What differentiates this part of the world from Scotland? Not the weather, nor the street names and generous use of tartan. These elements felt very Scottish. It was the wildlife that was so different from back home. In Scotland, we might have a few seals, but we do not have the world's smallest penguin and dolphin, rarest penguin and sea lion, and the world's only land-based Albatross colony. They are all here. We saw them all.

We knew that the thermal hotbed of the North Island would be fascinating. Geysers, mud pools, craters, beautiful and mysterious landscapes. And hot springs, great for the skin and the spirit.

After a flight back to Auckland, we toured around for a couple of weeks to see these natural wonders first hand. We soon got used to the omnipresent rotten egg-like smell of sulphur, as it pungently emerged from deep under the earth. It wasn't too bad once we stopped remembering it was there.

The area around the self-proclaimed capital of thermal New Zealand, Rotorua and nearby Lake Taupo, was certainly an epicentre of geothermal activity. We avoided the most obviously touristic attractions, including the place where they threw in soap powder to fire up the geyser for the crowds of naïve visitors. Such jiggery-pokery was hardly necessary, there were dramatic sights everywhere we went.

The wonderfully named Craters of the Moon, and the otherworldly Orakei Korako, provided great opportunities to appreciate these natural wonders. Steam rose in gusts and ribbon-like twirls, geysers gurgled and hissed, and ancient rocks reflected a fantastical kaleidoscope of colours. Given the obvious dangers in this outdoor chemistry laboratory, we took great care to ensure the kids did not wander off the carefully marked pathways. One misstep could have quickly turned a tripper into a cinder.

Although these places were not overly commercialised, there were a few holidaymakers. We hated the idea that we were tourists ourselves, even if this most definitely was not a holiday, apart from when it was. On occasions, we marvelled at the universality of the English language. We often heard people from different parts of the world chatting away in English, sometimes speaking it better than we could.

We based ourselves in Taupo for Rory's 11th birthday. This was another excuse for an accommodation upgrade, so we rented a luxury apartment for a couple of nights and within half an hour of checking in, doubled our stay. When you can watch TV, whilst sitting in a hot tub and looking out at the snowy mountains beyond Lake Taupo's shores, why would you move? The apartment had all sorts of mod cons and plenty of space. The kids both had that rare travel luxury, their own bedrooms, even though Rory's was essentially a walk-in wardrobe with a mattress on legs squeezed inside.

The complex even had a heated swimming pool. One afternoon, whilst taking a dip, Rory had a close shave with a duck which nearly flew into the back of his head. At the time, Roonagh did not realise how comical she was being when she shouted, "Rory, duck!"

Last up in this thermal wonderland was Hot Water Beach on the Coromandel Peninsula. This was precisely what the name suggested. Just choose your pitch, dig a hole in the sand and enjoy your own personal hot tub. But watch out for the extra hot water down there, you might get more than you bargain for, and end up like a packet of boil in the bag rice.

Our final night in New Zealand was spent in a small motel room high in the Auckland sky. We had a lot of re-packing to do in preparation for the last three months of our adventures.

Down below we could hear the strains of the US Rock Band, *The Killers*, who were playing a concert at the city's arena. We loved *The Killers* and desperately wanted to be at the gig. Sometimes there was a downside to travelling with kids. When what we wanted was *Mr Brightside*.

We left New Zealand with a tear in our collective eye. A 14 hour flight awaited to take us across the Pacific Ocean for the final continental leg of our year-long adventure. South America was waiting for us, and we were going to land just in time for the Easter Fiestas.

Caribbean Sea

SOUTH AMERICA

The Galapagos

Quito

Ecuador

The AMAZON

Peru

Brazil

Lima

Machu Pichu

Huacachina

Cuzco

Puno

RIO-UK

Colca Canyon

Arequipa

Bolivia

Copacabana

Rio de Janeiro

Santiago de Chile

N.Z.

Pajarito

Chile
What time is it?

Jetlag is a bit of a pain at any time. I had done my level best to construct an itinerary which minimised its impact. This time it was different. There was no way of avoiding it. We arrived in South America before we left New Zealand, or at least that is what our watches told us. Our bodies had no idea what was going on, other than that something was distinctly wrong.

We spent the entire Easter weekend in Santiago de Chile never once feeling quite right. In the end, the only way we managed to shift the jetlag was to fly five hours north and replace it with altitude sickness. What is it about jetlag that means you can't sleep, even though your body needs it more than anything else? Someone once told me that the only way to know you have cleared jetlag is when you wake up in the morning and your bodily functions are back where they should be. That didn't happen in Chile's capital city, Santiago.

Let's blame the jetlag for our arrival dramas at Santiago Airport. Bleary-eyed and disorientated, we didn't think to tick the box on the customs form which would have declared the small packet of raisins in our rucksack. Had we done that Anne would not have been hauled off like a criminal, an international contraband smuggler, by the excitable customs officials. With big guns, not of muscular variety. The penalty, non-negotiable even for such a small stash, was $200. Of course, we didn't have that in cash.

They frog-marched Anne to an ATM, conveniently positioned just outside their office. I suspect this was a common occurrence and remain fully confident that every cent found its way back to the Government. Maybe. Anne withdrew the cash, handed it over and off we slunk to the taxi rank. It was only then we discovered she had left her bank card in the ATM, the same card we had only been united with in Sydney two months previously. We travelled through South America with one bank card between us, just as we had most of Asia.

We were keen to experience Easter in South America. We imagined fantastical and colourful processions throughout Holy Week, with a myriad of photo opportunities and cultural insights. We booked our flight from New Zealand to Santiago to arrive the day before Good Friday.

We knew Santiago was one of the most westernised South American cities but had failed to appreciate that would also mean the most secular or least openly devout society. We discovered no colourful Easter processions or fiestas at all. We put our heads around the Cathedral door on Good Friday and had a walk around during the service. The place was only half full. Mainly Japanese tourists with camcorders, the mirror image of us in their temples a few months previously.

Blame the jetlag, blame Easter weekend, blame a lack of planning on my part. Whatever the reason, we left feeling we had not done Santiago justice. Our stay played an important role, allowing us to recover from the long flight and time difference. We didn't leave with strong memories of the city though, or any highlights to add to our list of the amazing things we had experienced during our year away.

It turned out Easter in Chile is pretty much like Easter at home, but without an egg hunt. Next stop was Quito in Ecuador, where apparently, they absolutely rock Easter. We arrived late on Easter Monday, just in time to miss it all.

Ecuador
Don't swim with piranhas

After nine months on the road, we needed a pause. Somewhere to call home for a while. But still a place which would be different and memorable. Quito, the capital city of Ecuador, fitted the bill. We found a cosy apartment on the edge of the largest and best-preserved colonial old town in South America. For three weeks the kids each had a bedroom, occasionally reliable internet, a tiny kitchen, a functioning washing machine and a balcony overlooking the Cathedral.

This was our first time at real altitude. As we stepped out of the airport into the cool Andean air, we gasped for breath. The air was so thin because we were 3,000 metres above sea level, that's nearly two miles high. Our apartment was on the fourth floor. It might as well have been on the 40th. We almost crawled up the stairwell on our hands and knees and literally fell into the front room, launching our faces into the welcome embrace of the living room sofa. Apart from Anne, who kept going straight to the bathroom and immediately threw up. She learnt something about herself during our couple of months in the Andes. Altitude and Anne were not best friends.

Although we used Quito as a launchpad for nature-based side trips, we mainly chose to hang out in the city. It was unlike anywhere we had been before, a proper traditional South American city.

Wide open squares were full of locals passing the time, reading a newspaper and having their shoes polished in the sunshine. The same squares were then stunningly floodlit at night in the cool mountain air. A church on every junction and a Nun around every corner. Armed police at every turn and pregnant women in every street.

Street sellers hawking whatever they could get their hands on as today's special. TV aerials, nappies, exhaust pipes, whatever really. The hourly arrival of Western or Asian tour groups, gasping for breath as they clicked their cameras at every turn. Ladies in traditional dress, not as a tourist attraction, which they were, but as their normal city attire for a trip from the countryside.

Toothless old men playing cards, smoking an endless chain of cigarettes. The sound of blind accordion players floating down the street. Cars hurtling past them with dogs perched on the roof, often wearing dog coats, just like in Japan. *Same same but different*. Trolleybuses rattling along the street, loudly playing *Rudolph the Red-Nosed Reindeer*. It was Easter, after all.

We had been warned about scams and were extra vigilant. One of the most frequent cons happened to us. A man in an upstairs flat tipped green paint out of his window onto my shoulder. A *helpful* stranger immediately appeared out of nowhere and started to wipe me down. "Here sir, please give me your camera so I can clean you up." No chance, I had read the guidebook and knew if I handed my camera over, he would be away on his heels before I could say "*Ayuda*."

One evening we took a taxi for a meal out. I think it was pizza, it usually was. We had done this ride a few times by now and knew the fixed fare was $2. When our driver asked for $3, I held firm and insisted he was only getting two. He was not happy, but I dug my heels in and slammed the taxi door as we fled into the restaurant. I explained to our waiter what had happened. Imagine my embarrassment when he told me that the fixed rate is indeed $2, in the daytime, and then rises to three in the evening. I so wanted to find that cabbie and pay him the full fare, plus interest. With hindsight, how tight was I, but that's what being on a restricted budget day after day can do to you.

Always on our list for South America, a trip into the Amazon Rainforest was bound to be a highlight. For a family who wanted to see animals, birds and habitats under threat from man, this was one special place. We chose to go to the Ecuadorian Amazon for two reasons. Partly cost, it was way cheaper than Peru, for example, but primarily because of Ecuador's fantastic biodiversity.

Ecuador is reputed to be one of the world's megadiversity hotspots. An estimated 40,000 plant species, 3,000 types of fish, 430 mammals and a staggering 2.5 million different kinds of insects. It has double the number of bird species of any one of Europe, North America or Australia. There are also 21 million human animals in the Amazon region. It's a busy old place.

Many of these humans are victims of man's systematic decimation of the Amazon. One and a half acres of rainforest disappears every second and 137 species become extinct each day. Remote tribes face the removal of their traditional way of life. Deforestation in the Amazon alone accounts for 30% of global carbon emissions. At this rate, there won't be any Amazon left in just 40 years. That's only half a human lifetime away.

We booked a five day trip to a lodge set on a lagoon in deep jungle. All it took was a half-hour plane hop across the Andes to the oil town of Lago Agrio, a bumpy two hour bus journey following the oil pipeline into the jungle, and then a two hour transfer on a motorised canoe. No carbon footprint there then.

During the canoe transfer, things seemed promising. A monkey fest ensued. Squirrel monkeys jumping across the trees to cross the river, marmosets hiding in the branches and cute little tamarin monkeys looking for their lunch.

The lodge was idyllic, set on the banks of the lagoon. In the shallows were caiman, relatives of our friend from the Borneo swimming pool. The sharp-toothed reptilians seemed less threatening in their natural environment. Squadrons of huge ants carried giant green leaves in a well-rehearsed military operation. Ants should come in *squadrons*, but maybe that's flying ants. The collective noun for ants is *army*, *colony*, or *swarm*. Or a *Soviet of ants*. Love the last one.

The dining hall came with its own boa constrictor, nestled innocently in the beams above our heads. The kids found this hilarious. On our first night, I had nightmares about this seductive serpent swallowing them whole. Actually, I don't think I dreamt it, that infers I slept. I lay in bed imagining it, playing the scene repeatedly in my head. When darkness fell in the heart of nature, the animal world awoke. The scratching of singing insects, the rustling of leaves, the far-off growls of jaguar all filled the jungle air. We had expected to do night-time hikes, but these were deemed too dangerous. If we had any doubt, it was dispelled by the beady eyes of snakes reflecting in the trees.

The only way in and out of the lodge was by canoe. The deep waters of the lagoon consisted predominately of rainwater. Our visit followed on from the rainy season when water fills the valley and rises to the top of the tallest trees. Without a shadow of doubt, the most magical time of day was sunset. The sky was ablaze with bright colours, yellow, orange, ochre, riotous red and finally rich purple. The surface was still, the air clear and blissfully free of mosquitoes which are unable to breed in this watery wonderland, the fallen leaves turning the water sufficiently acidic to prevent eggs from hatching.

This acidity did not deter marauding piranhas who swam beneath the surface of the lagoon. At sunset, boat loads of tourists would jump into the water for a pre-prandial dip. I never understood this, but at least it gave me something else not to sleep about at night. The kids loved the stories Mummy told them about "Other small beasties that live in the lagoon. They will swim up your bottom and live in your intestine for months." That helped me sleep as well.

Jungle life has the same addictive quality as an African safari. The tantalising knowledge that exotic fauna are close at hand and the desire to spot them, can become almost obsessive. This was fun for the kids for a while, but they quickly needed a reward to maintain their interest, positive affirmation that these zoo-like animals were really there.

Sightings were increasingly met with derision and disbelief. The bubbles on the water of a rare Pink River Dolphin. The alleged footprints of a snout-nosed Capybara. The scarcely believed utterances of a guide that there truly was "A three-toed sloth in a distant tree." But we did see those bubbles, nearly saw that Capybara, and I am convinced the sloth was visible. For the money we were spending I needed to.

The kids were craving time with little people of their own size. Opportunities for playmates had arisen in Australia during the Christmas holidays, but since then they had been their own social circle of two. A canoe trip to a riverside Amazonian community presented the possibility of hanging out with other kids for a while. Although this was only a brief stop, it was reminiscent of the innocent encounters they enjoyed in the Thai Hill Tribe village. Roonagh danced, skipped and ran with the local girls, and Rory kicked a ball about, delighted to have the opportunity to play football again for the first time in months.

Many excursions of this nature include some form of cooking, and this trip was no exception. We visited the small patch of land where all the village's vegetables were grown, dug up some yam and learnt how to make bread with it. Cooking the bread was easier than digging up the root in the first place. Think how long a yam is, that root takes some pulling up.

As for the incredible diversity of birdlife this particular corner of the Amazon promised? Well, we saw a solitary Toucan, and a few distant parrots one evening. We experienced much more exotic birdlife in Australia with its abundance of parrots, lorikeets and kookaburra. Perhaps, the Amazonian birds head elsewhere when the trees are submerged in acidic water. Makes sense when you have 2.5 million square miles to choose from. Nonetheless, this was disappointing for the kids, equipped with the *Guide to Amazonian Birds* we had purchased in Quito, which they had been studying hard.

The kids loved spending quality time in the Amazon Rainforest. As we made the reverse trip to Quito, they told us how lucky they felt.

"We know we are so fortunate to be spending this year in the world. Thank you for the opportunity to skip school for a year. We will remember this for the rest of our lives."

That was a great conversation.

Yet I needed some space. Any parent will recognise that feeling. When you are travelling together for a year, the emotion is multiplied many times. Especially if you are tired. After the bug-infested dreams of the jungle lodge, I was not as perky as I might have been.

One morning, I took myself off to a local Quito café for breakfast to write the Amazon blog. I looked up from my laptop as a dishevelled western family fell through the door. A mum, a dad, a boy and a girl. With wet hair and wearing t-shirts and swim shorts. I instantly deduced they were a travelling family, and all their clothes were probably in the laundry. Sure enough, they were Kiwis over-landing from Mexico City to Chile. These guys were hardcore, using buses to work their way down Central and South America. The girl was the same age as Roonagh and the 12 year old boy was called Rory.

We arranged to visit the vibrant Saturday market at Otavalo, a couple of hours away deep in the Andes. The animal market was chaotic, pitiful puppies in cardboard boxes, chirping chicks scooped up into brown paper bags, everything was for sale. The main market spilled out from the Town Square into many of the adjoining streets. We made a few choice purchases, jewellery, wall hangings and a jazzy poncho for Roonagh. We had reached the stage of the trip where we could start buying things for home.

Our Kiwi companions would remember this day, in the same way I still shudder at the thought of sitting in the Elephant Café in Chiang Mai. Just as I lost our photos of Bangkok and Cambodia, they had a calamity with their pictures of Central America, Colombia and Northern Ecuador. Not because of hard drive failure but at the hands of a pickpocket. The parents had commented on the way to Otavalo that they needed to upload their photos from their camera's memory card. They never got the chance. It was swiped from their daughter's backpack as they shopped. I still feel their pain to this day. And her heartbreak in particular.

On our return journey, we made a brief stop at Mitad del Mundo, *Middle of the World*, on the Equator. We stood in a line for a photo opportunity, each of us with one foot in each hemisphere. Two families, one from Scotland and the other from New Zealand, meeting each other halfway around the world. How's that for bookends?

Galápagos Islands
One snorkel too many

"You're not going to the Galápagos? That's crazy. There's no way we are missing out on that."

How envious were we of our new friends, this intrepid family from New Zealand. Having to remove this dream destination from our itinerary for financial reasons still hurt. Especially for a family supposed to be having a trip based on seeing as many endangered animals and places as possible. Our anguish became increasingly excruciating as we walked around Quito. One of the main reasons Ecuador made it on to our schedule was as a gateway to the Galápagos. There were reminders everywhere. T-shirts, fridge magnets, posters, pretty much every form of tourist tat known to man. Our wildlife experience in the Amazon simply made us feel the pain more. We had a taste and wanted to indulge in the full menu.

But it turned out our friends weren't going on an expensive cruise. I had erroneously thought that was the only option. They figured we could all get a flight to one of the islands and take it from there.

"All we need to do is find a local captain at the port of the main town and charter his small boat. A few hundred dollars, split between two families. Why don't you join us?"

We did some sums, figured it might just work and took a gamble. Three days later we all stepped off the plane to start our week-long Galápagos adventure.

What an adventure it was. After pounding the pavements, we figured that a boat charter was beyond our means even at last-minute prices. However, there were plenty of short trips readily available. We based ourselves for four nights in the capital island, Santa Cruz, spent two nights on the largest island, Isabella and took a day trip to nearby Floreana, home of the world's most famous tortoise, Lonesome George.

The Galápagos is an archipelago of volcanic islands on the Equator, 1,000 kilometres east of Ecuador in the Pacific Ocean. Famous for its giant tortoises, it remains one of the places on earth most untouched by man. Charles Darwin's visit in 1835 is reputed to have inspired the Theory of Evolution.

Although 97% of the island is a national park, the introduction of non-native creatures such as goats, rats and domestic animals has caused widespread damage, pushing many species to the brink of extinction. Native tortoises took a big hit from early explorers. They could be kept alive in a ship for up to 100 days without needing food or water and were then slaughtered for their meat and oil.

We saw none of this human impact on our visit. The Galápagos Islands were our only animal-based destination where nature had not only been left to do its thing but was also actively conserved. We had seen plenty of conservation projects in places where man had pushed exotic creatures and habitat to the brink of extinction. But not here, not in this journey through an old David Attenborough programme. Documentaries filmed in a world before forest fires, illegal logging and the filling of the oceans with plastic.

Here was a child-friendly treasure trove of wildlife, where the kids could get up close and personal with giant tortoises, marine iguanas and even swim with sea lions. There were species which could not be found anywhere else, or at least not so close at hand. The uniqueness of the Galápagos is not just this cornucopia of animals and birds, it is that they aren't bothered about us. We are just a particularly peculiar hairless mammal.

Yet these waters, like any other ocean, hide danger. In this case, the choppy waves themselves. Set deep in the wilds of the Pacific Ocean, they must not be under-estimated. We had another near-fatal incident involving one of the kids. This time Roonagh. She nearly drowned whilst snorkelling with sea lions.

It was an overcast and slightly breezy afternoon. The boat carried us an hour or so from port, dropped its anchor, and we slipped into our wetsuits. Roonagh and I that is, the other family members didn't fancy it. Fools to miss out on this, I thought. There was no way Roonagh and I were going to turn our noses up at this once in a lifetime opportunity. After all, who gets to snorkel with sea lions, in the Galápagos Islands?

In we jumped, 200 metres from the pebble beach. The boat couldn't safely moor any nearer given the preponderance of jaggy rocks in the bay. We started to swim towards the shallows, where our guide told us young sea lions would be frolicking. Initially Roonagh and I were close to each other, but then currents started to push us apart. She was wearing a lifejacket and I wasn't unduly worried. I had other priorities. I am not a strong swimmer and was giving my feeble breaststroke a significant part of my attention.

Suddenly there were the sea lions, swimming towards me, around me and under me. I started snorkelling and snapping away with my underwater camera. It was a joyous and timeless experience. Like nothing else I had ever done. They swam towards me, rolling, turning and grinning as if they had been waiting for this moment all their lives. They were so pleased to see me, and me them.

Unbeknown to me, things were not going as swimmingly for Roonagh. She was now 100 metres away and in difficulty. She had drifted to the left and the rip was dragging her towards precipitous rocks. Anne was watching horrified from the boat, her daughter's life flashing before her eyes. Just as I had been when Rory nearly cycled under that bus in China. Except this moment wasn't over in a flash, it got worse. Every time the ocean swelled, Roonagh's bobbing head disappeared behind a huge wave. Each time this happened, Anne feared her daughter would not reappear as the wave subsided.

Fortunately, the tour guide was alert to this. A strong, tanned man, he powered towards her, like a torpedo fired from a nuclear submarine, and quickly cradled her in his arms. He then brought her over to me.

"Where have you been Roonagh?"

Roonagh joined in the sea lion gymnastics, stirred but unscathed by her near miss. Anne too survived the experience of what was for her the worst day of the entire trip.

Then there was the time we feared our boat would capsize. We were halfway through an inter-island transfer on a small and well-loaded vessel. Think water taxi more than boat. With 30 passengers on board and no life jackets. Suddenly, in the middle of the ocean, with no land in sight, the captain cut the engine. And lit a cigarette.

We sat puzzled for a few minutes and then noticed a similar boat, both in size and passenger numbers, drifting towards us. It transpired its engine had failed. *Water Taxi the Second* gently bumped into us, and its perplexed passengers jumped on board. We all shuffled up and off we headed, the hull of this tiny craft slightly more submerged as we puttered our way towards our destination. Then we stopped again. This time for a brilliant reason.

It was a sea life scene like none we had ever seen before. A feeding frenzy. Something straight out of a nature documentary, minus the dramatic music and charismatic commentary. We had already seen plenty of dolphins, sea lions and sea birds by this stage of the trip. But never all engaged in a feast at the same time. No doubt below the water there were also shoals of sharks engaged in a dramatic ballet with their marine companions.

Masked Boobies carpet-bombed the churning waves in their thousands, diving several metres into the deep to avail themselves of the plentiful fish being chased and consumed by the dolphins and sea lions. The sharks no doubt had their eyes on larger prizes, but fortunately we didn't witness that gory spectacle.

The irony, we had previously paid good money to head out on water-based wildlife tours, with mixed results. Yet here we were, basically on a local bus, dangerously overloaded and breaching many health and safety rules, witnessing one of nature's greatest dramas, all for a few dollars.

On another boat trip, we witnessed the mating routine of the frigate bird. These amorous seafarers, familiar to mariners of yesteryear, hence the name, were in residence in the Galápagos. When they mate, the male inflates the red pouch on his neck, much like the balloon on the end of an old-fashioned blood pressure monitor. It swells to the size of a children's party balloon. One of our group, an eight year old girl who had clearly been paying attention in Biology class back home, became most animated.

"They're mating, they're mating," she shouted several times. Her parents looked mortified and probably grateful they weren't in a monkey forest, farmyard or any other location where animals do what comes naturally.

Understandably, the quality of internet connection was not of the highest standard in the Galápagos Islands. In some ways, this was refreshing, although no doubt this will change as time goes by and progress continues unabated. But try telling that to an 11 year old Manchester United fanatic whose team are playing in the second leg semi-final of the Champions League whilst a feeding frenzy is happening in the water in front of him. The marine banquet was successful in taking his mind off all matters football related. However, once we docked and checked into our overnight accommodation, he was more than impatient to learn if his team had reached the final. To be fair, so was his father.

The small fishing hamlet did have a corner shop with a single computer terminal. We headed there and patiently waited our turn. Having fed the meter, I waited for the dial-up internet to reveal our destiny. Younger readers won't remember dial-up internet. Imagine having the news typed for you live, one word at a time.

It must have taken at least ten minutes, ten long torturous minutes, for the page to load. It was worth the wait. We had won and were heading to Rome for the Champions League Final on 27th May. We were going to Rome, the Eternal City. Well, we weren't obviously because we were 7,000 miles away, but our team of superstars in red were. I quickly checked our itinerary. We would be in Peru, but I did not know where. Other than we would be in front of a TV screen. We weren't going to miss that match and find out the result by dial-up.

Isabella Island is home to the Sierra Negra volcano. Not any old volcano, this beauty has the second largest crater in the world, a mind-boggling eight miles wide. That's one heck of a lot of lava when she blows, which she had done just four years previously. We rode up the slopes on horseback, stopping occasionally to admire wildflowers thriving in the rich volcanic soil, or play in lava tubes carved into the wilderness by the fires which burned beneath our feet.

It was another worldly landscape, like no other we had witnessed. One of our party was German, and I asked if he had ever seen anything like it before?

"Yes," he replied curtly, "last year on a package holiday to Lanzarote."

That put me in my place, we were all this way from home, yet he was telling me we could have just hopped on a cheap flight to the Canary Islands and had the same experience.

Sorry, but I don't think so, I thought, as we observed the flumes of smoke billowing from the latest Galápagos island being born just a few miles away.

The Galápagos Islands, nature in full technicolour and in the making. What a wonderland. We saw it close at hand, not from a cruise liner. It's funny how things work out, if I hadn't spied that family in their board-shorts in a coffee shop in Quito we would never have gone. If I hadn't messed up our budget, we would have been already, but on a ridiculously expensive cruise ship. Serendipity. Got to love it.

Peru
Who would want to be a Guinea Pig?

It was not serendipity we spent a month in Peru. That was always the plan, no matter what else changed. What a great decision, we loved Peru. The colour, the history, the people, the scenery, the sights.

Stumbling off the early morning plane in Cuzco, we were greeted by a scene straight out of the classic 1990s TV comedy sketch series, *The Fast Show*. A troupe of Peruvian troubadours, dressed in full traditional garb and brandishing a wide array of musical instruments, including the ubiquitous panpipes, welcomed bleary-eyed visitors with a rendition of *El Condor Pasa*. A tune we were to hear at least twice daily during our month-long sojourn in Peru. They seemed to be unsuccessful in selling any CDs, but unabashed, they soon picked up their gear and moved onto the next baggage carousel ready to pounce on the next herd of tourists.

Walking into the main square in Cuzco, we instantly knew this was the South America we had always imagined. The vibrancy, the living history, the very feel of the place. Cuzco is the tourist or "*Gringo*" as locals call them, capital of South America, as evidenced by the plethora of Irish and British bars around the Plaza de Armas. However, it is still quintessentially Peruvian. As a pal of ours said, "*Cuzco Rocks.*"

Let's deal with the Gringo aspect first. Most tourists come to Cuzco to visit Machu Picchu and the Sacred Valley. A certain vibrancy comes from having tourists staying for just a day or two to see the sights. Or alternatively, just hanging out whilst recovering from a trek. Cuzco has laid on everything they need. Outdoor shops for trekkers, more agencies than can be viable, more happy hours than can possibly be drunk and what seems like thousands of souvenir stores.

A welcoming expat community thrives in the city. We dived in through the highly recommended South American Explorers Clubhouse and Jack's Café, the best value food of our entire year. Cuzco is a warm and welcoming place. And if you're interested in *piktures*, *chompers* or *massajes* it's definitely your destination of choice. Maintaining a running score of how many offers of each we got kept the kids entertained on our daily march to Jack's Café through the cold early evening air.

Cuzco is very photogenic. The setting, the light, the colours and the characters combine to form a rich tapestry upon which photographers way better than we can weave their magic. You can even, for a *soles* or two, have your photo taken with a dressed-up lamb, kid (goat or human), alpaca or llama, wizened old lady in traditional costume, or even an Inca Prince.

"Tandoori Guinea Pig anyone? Jeez no, look away kids."

Guinea pigs may be cute pets, but we didn't fancy eating them for lunch. No matter how many times we were asked. Even in *cuyerias*, restaurants designed specifically for the purpose, where every dish on the menu contains the said rodent, the *cuy*. We even drove through a village where every single restaurant specialised in all dishes guinea pig. The second Friday in October is even the National Day of the Cuy. Fortunately, we arrived in May.

The area around Cuzco, our on-off base for the month, is characterized by tourists as an Inca Theme Park, with every justification. For this truly is the Land of the Incas and the evidence is very much all around. Not just in the remains of outstanding buildings and civilizations, but still living in the local people's faces, the Quechua language they still speak, the festivals and ceremonies they have, the clothes they wear and the culture they still celebrate. A proud Cuscueno today is still very much a proud Inca.

The Incas came to prominence in the Cuzco area in the 12th century and spawned a long line of Inca Kings who ruled this region, undertaking great works and a cultural revolution. Only when the 9th King, Pachacutec came to the throne, did the Inca empires expand. Within just 25 years a rapid military expansion led to the conquering of much of the Andes, a span of 3,000 kilometres.

This new empire became known as the *Land of Four Quarters*, signified by the flag which still flies over Cuzco today and conquered the areas, peoples and cultures from Colombia all the way down to Chile. They subjugated the entire Andes chain, top to bottom, including the Andean parts of Bolivia and northern Argentina. Anyone who has travelled around South America will appreciate this is a massive and challenging terrain.

The invading Spanish routed the empire in 1532, converting the last Inca King to Christianity and then executing him one year later. And bagging one heck of a lot of gold in the process. The Spanish sacked and pillaged much of what they found. That is why Inca sites are now ruins, rather than due to the lengthy passage of time.

One of the things I loved most about South America was that problems were no longer my fault as a Brit. The colonial chip fell from my shoulder. Every time the kids had asked why a particular atrocity or injustice occurred in history, I had tended to answer, "*because we did it*." The British Empire that is. From South Africa to Australia, via many parts of Asia, it was our responsibility. Blame only occasionally deflected by the legacy of French or Dutch rule.

But here in South America, the blame could be squarely laid at the Spanish Empire's feet, apart from when it was the Portuguese's fault. It was liberating, albeit not as much as their eventual independence must have been for these proud indigenous races. They left a great legacy for us to explore, so we did.

The most significant treasure trove of Inca sites is *La Valle Sagrada*, the Sacred Valley, the dramatic Inca heartland just outside Cuzco. There was a well-established day trip which took in many of the highlights. We devoured it in bite-size pieces.

A shared minibus drove us to the Sunday market in the picturesque town of Chinchero, bustling with women in traditional costumes, men with pipes and the cutest children in the world. And popcorn, big buckets of popcorn, costing just a few *soles,* so the kids were permitted to stuff their faces.

We also hired a driver to visit Las Salineras, where the Incas filled their pots with salt from the saline saturated hillsides. He also took us to the stunning agricultural terracing and ruined mountain citadel at Pisac. It was a foretaste of the wonders we would see at the world-renowned Machu Picchu in a couple of weeks, and we couldn't wait.

Roonagh stayed in the car at Las Salineras and Pisac. She could not walk. This was not courtesy of the over consumption of popcorn, but due to childhood over-exuberance of a different kind.

We had done well in avoiding injury on our travels. Ok, Rory fell through a window in South Africa, and there was the odd injured knee, tropical disease and near-death experience. But, given the potential for things to go wrong in a year of travel, it was a decent record. With less than a month to go, a trip to the ancient archaeological attraction of Moray seemed unlikely to threaten our safety record.

Picture a ridged concentric bowl set deep into the earth, like an upturned Royal Albert Hall. Each layer two to three metres deep, with four stone steps set into each terrace. The Incas used this site as a research centre for potato cultivation. Each terrace was set at a different altitude to establish the optimum growing height for various varieties. Like an Inca Greenhouse.

As their parents gingerly made their way down, the kids scampered ahead, and Rory took the opportunity to do backward leaps at the bottom, his sister assuming the role of paparazzi. A couple of minutes later, their breathless and reckless Dad suggested, "Why don't you both jump off the bottom step, it would make an awesome photo."

In my defence, I had not yet appreciated this was a two metres leap.

Rory went first, no problem. Roonagh then had a go. Everything looked fine as she leapt through the air. However, the piercing screams which followed, echoing around the bowl and into the thin blue air would have made you think the Incas were making a human sacrifice to their Gods. Looking at her lying prostrate in the base of the bowl we were clearly leaving the Land of the Incas in an air ambulance and heading home to have her ankle reset, the trip brought to a premature end.

Out of nowhere, half a dozen burly workmen appeared. They were working on renovations. They should have been installing safety railings and warning signs so we wouldn't have faced this predicament. No doubt discomforted by their dereliction of duty, they took it in turns to give Roonagh a piggyback up to the top of the bowl. I lagged breathlessly behind, feeling very guilty.

We were taken straight to a small hut where the world seemed to throng around the injured child. She was a celebrity for the morning. To this day, she is pleased she had at least painted her toenails the previous evening. A large bandage appeared and then, in this most rural of locations, the accident book. There may not have been barriers or hazard notices, but at least there was some semblance of health and safety provision. Perhaps children nearly die here all the time. The book was somewhat full.

Our driver then whisked us off to the nearest town where, by a process of osmosis, he located the local "*doctor,*" a farmer on his way back from the fields. We were taken down a lane into the backyard of a house where the farming physician's family were preparing lunch.

Dr Farmer removed the bandage, applied something which looked like liquid poo, followed by a dressing made from ripped newspaper. Our driver assured us that the liquified sewage was perfectly safe, a traditional remedy known as *siete hierbas*, seven herbs in English.

Roonagh spent the rest of the day in my arms, and we cancelled our planned three day trek into the Inca countryside. That night's sleep was very restless, for her and us. Would we have to bring forward our return to the UK or just transfer to the nearest hospital? How infected would the liquid poo make her leg?

The following afternoon she started running and then leaping. I don't know what was in that murky concoction, but I would like to get my hands on some. Not literally, of course. But I am sure there is a gap in the market for such an effective product, although it would need creative advertising given the way it looked.

Our Cuzco-based Inca pilgrimage's final component was a trip to the substantial ruins that lie just outside the city. We took an early morning taxi out to the furthest site at Tambomachay and called in at the others as we walked the 12 kilometres back to the city. The most impressive was the massive Inca fort of Sacsaywaman, pronounced *Sexy Woman*, although it actually means *Satisfied Falcon*. Even though only one fifth of the original site remains, the Spanish having used it as a quarry, this place is immense and sits majestically above the city. It was almost as impressive as the gang of taxi drivers playing a full-on football match in the mid-morning heat at 3,400 metres altitude. Cuzco is home to the world's highest Irish Bar. No doubt that was their next stop.

Cuzco boasts one of the top football teams in Peru. One Saturday afternoon Rory and I decided to catch a game, keen to make up for our failed attempt in Yokohama.

The ground was a taxi ride away. Turning the corner, I hailed a cab and asked the driver to take us to the stadium. He asked me if I knew what the score was? I was puzzled, it was only 2:00 pm.

"No, señor, you do not understand, the match was this morning. Cusco won three goals to zero."

Thanking him, we quickly turned around, knowing that yet another matchday was not meant to be.

Rather like Asia with its temples, there was a danger of getting Inca'd out in this stunningly beautiful part of the world. Especially for kids, after a while each site started to look like the last. We were lucky we had time to space things out and chill on down days. We needed energy in our tank for the magical Peruvian delights still to come.

Ok, so it is touristy. A trip to Lake Titicaca, the world's highest inland navigable lake, features in pretty much every *Highlights of Peru* itinerary.

To be honest, it's a lake. A large body of water at altitude. We are fortunate to come from a country with many such stunningly beautiful expanses, the wonderful Scottish lochs.

So, beyond being a lofty lake, what else is Titicaca? We decided to allocate a week of our month in Peru to find out.

Well, first there was a long, but beautiful, journey from Cuzco. Ten hours on the *Inca Express*, the high class and high cost, tourist bus traversing a stunning stretch of the Andes, reaching a whopping 4,500 metres at its highest pass. Just shy of three miles high in the sky. Anne was still struggling with altitude sickness and would have been grateful if an oxygen mask had fallen from above her seat, like in an in-flight emergency. The kids loved it though, especially Rory, who had become quite the photographer during our travels. Alpacas set against a backdrop of snow-capped mountains and glaciers, now there's a screensaver.

As the bus pulled in at dusk, first impressions of Titicaca were not promising. Arrival at the principal town on the Peruvian side, Puno, saw us pitching up in a large commercial port town. The main tourist area was a taxi ride from the lakeside, and to be honest, the whole place was a bit of a dump.

The quality of the food was also poor. As vegetarians, we accept our menu choices will always be limited, and we had eaten more than our fair share of pizza by this point, but this stuff was rank. Even the Chinese do better pizza.

After checking into our Fawlty Towers style hotel, our first job was to book a bus ticket to move on again the next morning. We were not planning on leaving Lake Titicaca though. There was a side trip we did not want to miss out on. Bolivia was only three hours away by bus.

Bolivia
Watch out for the nachos

Lake Titicaca sits between Peru and Bolivia. There are no ferries across, so you have to take the road. Whether you are making a side trip as we did or carrying on to La Paz and beyond.

We headed for the main Bolivian lake-based town, a wee place called Copacabana. Not the last Copacabana we would visit during the dying embers of our time in South America. And hardly deep into Bolivia. About 30 minutes' drive from the border. But still in Bolivia, our 20th country of the trip.

Lake Titicaca sits at 3,800 metres above sea level on the Peruvian side, and 3,900 metres above sea level in Bolivia. I don't think it slopes, my rudimentary grasp of physics suggests not. At night-time, the temperature plummeted. The cold was intense the moment the sun dipped into the lake. Hot water bottles were even on sale. The contrast between t-shirt day-time weather and what felt, by comparison, to be Arctic nights, was a real shock to the system.

Anne and I celebrated our wedding anniversary in Copacabana. Barry Manilow even wrote a song for us.

With a local babysitter organised for the kids, we hit the town and found a romantic hillside restaurant that sloped even more than the lake. We ordered the only vegetarian option, Nachos. Our waitress delivered a small packet of Doritos and a jar of gloopy cheese sauce which must have contained more E numbers than the Oxford English Dictionary. As I looked down the hill and over the table at Anne, holding the jar tight so it would not propel itself directly over her head and straight into the street, I felt like the luckiest man alive.

Copacabana is a quiet place, a local town for local people. Travellers pass through, maybe staying for a night to take a trip out on the lake the following morning. We were lucky to arrive on Sunday, always the best day to catch locals having fun anywhere in the world.

The whole town seemed to be engaged in what looked like a mass wedding ceremony. There were cars dressed in garlands and ribbons everywhere and what looked like a wedding fayre up near the church. It transpired this was a traditional ceremony where locals bring their new cars to get blessed and then get absolutely hammered. No one could tell us how many centuries back this automobile-based tradition stretched.

We had fun watching revellers party in the late afternoon sun. Large women in bowler hats played football in front of lakeside stalls selling barbecued fish. Children rode horses along the beach and boats bobbed along the shoreline.

They like their women large in Bolivia. Really large. The bigger, the better. Hefty. Apparently, on her wedding day, the bride wears 16 petticoats to make herself even bigger and therefore more irresistible, to her new husband. Bowler hat and pipe are optional. For the groom.

Our main activity on the Bolivian side of Titicaca was a trip to the legendary La Isla del Sol, believed by the Incas to be the birthplace of the sun. For tuppence halfpenny, we took the slow ferry over for an afternoon excursion. We had been on many boats by this point and this felt like just another one to the kids.

"Dad, can we play Uno, this boat is boring."

In reality it was stunning, sparkling water juxtaposed with the snow-capped Bolivian mountains glistening in the distance. I guess your excitement threshold is high when you've been on the road for 11 months. Especially when you are 9 or 11 years old.

Our time on La Isla del Sol was brief and exhausting. The 100 steps up from the harbour nearly gave me a cardiac arrest. It's dangerous to forget you are three miles high when you're trying to keep up with your mountain goat-like son. I feared my chest would explode.

"Come on Dad, keep up."

It was just as well I did not have the lung capacity to reply, for my response would not have been child friendly.

The lake is a deeply spiritual place. Revered by the Incas, it hosted many religious ceremonies. Therefore, it was appropriate, albeit unintentional, that Anne made a sacrifice to the Gods. Her £350 Gucci prescription sunglasses tipping off her head as we disembarked back in Copacabana, tumbling silently into the waters below. I hope the Gods were grateful.

Peru
Flying high

Upon our return to Puno, we had two priorities. Organising a non-touristy trip to experience the lives and culture of the people living on and around Lake Titicaca. And finding a venue to watch the Champions League Final between our team, Manchester United and the South Americans' favourites, Barcelona.

Let's get the painful second item quickly out the way. At 1:45 pm local time we sat down with pints, kids' cocktails and takeaway pizza in a Reggae Bar, encouragingly called *Positive Rock*. The locals were out in force, all in Barcelona shirts. The banter was fun, and the omens looked good.

For the first nine minutes of the match, United played out of their skins and looked odds on to become the first team to retain the Champions League trophy. Imagine that, European Champions when we left the UK and still champions when we got home. You don't need me to tell you what happened next. If you do, well I'm not going to. Ask Google.

The worst thing was, when the match was over, we couldn't just call it a night and head to bed, feeling better in the morning. It was a long afternoon in Puno.

We were more successful in organising a bespoke two day eco trip to take us to places most tourists don't venture, as well as those they do.

Fuelled by a 5:00 am breakfast buffet laid on especially for us, we were driven 45 minutes into the Altiplano. Spanish for *high plain*, the Altiplano is the largest area of plateau on earth outside of Tibet.

As dawn broke, we rowed over to an island for a VIP tour. Exotic wildlife abounded, vizcachas (a rabbit-like relative of the racoon), vicuñas (posh relatives of llamas and alpacas) and a black-chested buzzard eagle.

Next stop was a clamber up a hillside to see *Chulpas*, ancient pre-Inca funeral towers. At this point, I would love to share some highlights of the history lesson we received. Because I had said "*hola*" on arrival, our guide, Wilma, was under the misconception I spoke, or at least understood, rapid Spanish. I did my best, but much of the, presumably fascinating, history was lost on us.

We were then taken to our home for the next 18 hours, a homestay experience with a local farmer. Juan, his wife Isabella and their eight year old daughter Milli lived in what, by local standards, was probably a mansion. Their small farm, just outside the nearest town, had several outbuildings and some land. They owned several llamas and alpacas, including one rather frisky boy called *Pepe* who made a valiant effort to increase the group's size through the amorous activities he was engaged in when we arrived. The sandy courtyard also included several guinea pigs, not pets, and a dog with four puppies, hopefully pets.

Juan and Isabella made us feel welcome. Their home-cooked food was superb, with creative and extensive use of home-grown quinoa. The kids enjoyed having fun with the puppies and playing football, volleyball and other local games. They also loved taking a baby alpaca for a walk. I also had a turn at being dragged across the Altiplano by this surprisingly strong young fellow.

With hindsight, we wish we had done more of this type of activity. It was fascinating and humbling to stay with a local family and experience their way of life in an environment so different from our privileged existence. The kids also benefitted from spending time with children their own age from such different circumstances.

We hunkered down for the night in the small, detached guest room set at the back of the farmstead. I suspect the alpacas were somewhat peeved at being displaced for the night.

It was the coldest night of our lives. The last occasion I had experienced similar indoor temperatures was the first time Anne brought me to Edinburgh for Hogmanay, and we stayed in her friend's unheated student flat. We slept in two single beds, one child and adult per bed, under layers of alpaca-wool blankets and draped in heavy ponchos. In Peru I mean, not Edinburgh.

After almost no sleep, a hearty breakfast awaited us before we were driven to Puno harbour for our second day's activities.

A day on the lake. A perfect way to follow our night in the homestay and round off our week around Lake Titicaca.

A short boat ride took us to the world-renowned Uros Islands. The floating islands are constructed from reeds which grow in the lake. As they rot in the water, new layers are placed on top.

We were somewhat nervous, knowing that this is one of the most touristy experiences in the whole of Peru. Hassle central, with many scams. Some of the floating islands were allegedly fakes, not somewhere where the islanders live, but a place they only go to entertain tourists before returning home to relative comfort on the mainland each evening.

We saw none of that, having taken great care to sign up with an operator offering *non-touristy trips*. An oxymoron perhaps, like the wealthy beggar or miserly philanthropist.

We were taken, as a group of four, not fifty, to two separate islands. The villagers took great care and delight in explaining their way of life and customs through an interpreter. We were impressed to see solar panels in place on some of their homes.

The dress was, typically for this region, very colourful and the children were ultra-cute. The only thing about the experience we would change is not having a group of women and children sing us off the island. The first rendition was at least a traditional tune, but they let themselves down by following it with *Twinkle Twinkle Little Star*. In English. Perhaps the *non-touristy trip* was a little touristy after all.

Our cruiser for the day was somewhat overkill. We were the only passengers, so did not need two guides, two crew and twenty seats. But the latter came in useful. After our sleepless night in the Alpaca Shed, we were ready for some shut-eye. The guides and crew must have been perplexed to see their four paying passengers lying prostrate across rows of chairs, fast asleep as they safely carried us across the lake to the remote Llachon peninsula.

Each lakeside community had its own dress and local customs. We wanted to experience some of this off the beaten track. We headed to an area which does not feature on the tourist trail. The tour provider promised lunch with a local family. It was something of a disappointment to discover we were booked into a family-run restaurant with a group of American tourists. Sometimes it's impossible to escape the gringo trail.

Following a post-prandial walk back to the boat, we had a siesta on board as our trusty crew took us back to grotty old Puno. The next day, as we took an eight hour bus back to Cuzco, we had the opportunity to reflect on an excellent trip to Lake Titicaca. A unique part of South America, accessible for tourists, but still so far removed from the world in which we live. Well worth allocating two percent of our total trip time.

By Rory, aged 11.

Up at 4 o'clock in the morning, what in the world could be worse but try and think of a better thing to do today than explore the lost Inca city of Machu Picchu. We got the bus to Machu Picchu with all the other backpackers who had read the Lonely Planet. But at the ruins the tourists spread out and you could instantly hear the chattering of the thousands of blue and white swallows. Instead of rushing frantically around the ruins we started to climb steep steps and then we let ourselves take in Machu Picchu, a view that will be with me like a postcard at the bottom of a mailbox and it will stay always deep down inside. A place of dreams.

We climbed higher, the Mitred Parakeets flew higher and the sun rose higher and over the hills a stunning sight. The sun stayed high as we walked down and the ruins were also high, above our expectations, wandering down the hallways of the past to walk through doors to see the young llamas and playful little rabbits hopping and skipping around the grassy courtyards.

We stayed at Peru's show site for 5 and half hours or I should probably say the show site of South America. We sadly departed this, the jewel of South America, and a doughnut was shared and a few Cokes were gulped down at the café.

Machu Picchu means *Old Mountain* in Quechua, the ancient Inca language still spoken in these parts today. The train journey to this old mountain, or more precisely to Aguas Calientes, the tourist town nestled in a valley below, is reputed to be one of the world's most stunning train rides. We knew that by the price of the glass-fronted observation carriage. We opted for the more affordable second-class ticket. It was just as well.

During our 90 minute taxi ride to catch the train from Ollantaytambo, my stomach started to feel discombobulated.

Anne and I had enjoyed a lovely meal the previous evening, a second attempt at celebrating our wedding anniversary. We had even had a glass of wine, but just one. At altitude, even small quantities of alcohol create hangovers that would fell a giant. I had woken with a slight headache but nothing worse. But as we neared the train station, I felt distinctly unwell. The wine was not to blame.

We had opted not to take the deluxe tourist bus back from Puno to our home base in Cuzco. In the chaos of the busy bus station, I had failed to get us on a tourist coach. We found ourselves ensconced on a local bus which stopped frequently in every market town. And this was a Saturday, so every town had a market. The only saving grace was that the bus had a toilet. When I say toilet, I mean a hole in the floor. Even that was preferable to one toilet Anne and Roonagh paid a couple of *soles* to use in a bus station en route. They were quicker out of there than a Guinea Pig in a KFC.

When I needed a pee, I stood up, unaware the bus was pulling into a market square where the entire population could stop to stare through the open window, in awe I like to think, as I did my business.

What does this have to do with Machu Picchu? Well, my hand hygiene on the journey must not have been of pandemic standards. As we arrived at a souvenir shop near the train station, I dived into the toilet at the back and sat down very quickly. What ensued was not pleasant.

"Ok Anne, grab the kids, we're leaving."

Our South African shopkeeper back in Kwazulu-Natal would not have been impressed.

As we stood outside the train station, I promptly vomited over a bridge into the babbling Andean river water below. And then spent the entire train journey, one of the most impressive in the world, in the toilet with my head alternately between the bowl and the floor.

We arrived at our hotel in the early afternoon and I went straight to bed. I was wiped out, groaning in a single bed, apart from when my bowels convulsed so much that I had to dash to the small room next door.

Anne entertained the kids in local cafés, shops and markets. It was like being back in Borneo. Only this time, I didn't have the luxury of days to recover. We had one night in Aguas Calientes and one chance to see the sunrise over Machu Picchu. As the hours passed, it became increasingly evident I would miss this once in a lifetime opportunity. When Anne and the kids returned to the room at bedtime, I announced that they would have to go without me in the morning. I had rarely felt so low.

Then at 1:00 am, I started to feel slightly better. I drank some water, popped a couple of pills, nibbled on a slice of bread and got some sleep. The alarm clock rang at 4:00 am.

"Everybody up, it's time to get the bus to Machu Picchu."

It was all worthwhile as we stood arm in arm as a family, watching the sun rise over the old mountain and cast golden shadows on the ancient stone ruins laid out in front of our eyes.

Let's leave the final words on this magical day to Roonagh:

One of the many fantastic days of the trip was ahead. It was a short but twisty bus ride up to the entry to the Machu Picchu Sanctuary. There was a big queue to get in. We rushed up some steep staircases. When we got our first view of the magnificent 7th Wonder of the World, Machu Picchu.

Although it was still a little bit dark it was still amazing to see it. We got all our pictures taken before all the people got in. Then we walked along a path to an Inca bridge but first it was me and Mum who turned around but the boys came back about ten minutes later. We sat down for a bit and admired the views. We also got a bonus because of lots of snowy mountains behind us. After that we walked down on the terracing to a small hut and we took lots of photos. Then we walked down to the main ruins of the fantastic site.

First we saw the 3 windowed temple. After that we walked through hidden doorways and the temple of the condor. I took photos of Spotty on Inca walls. We sat on the side for a bit looking at the long line of terracing running up the mountain. A refreshment at the café was nice. We went in one more time to say goodbye to Machu Picchu. We got the bus back and we had lunch at a café with a parrot in it.

Arequipa. Two days in Peru's second largest city, a launching point for the Colca Canyon and a trip to see condors. We stepped off the night bus from Cuzco at 5:30 am with bleary eyes and backpacks bulging with souvenirs and *chompas*, knowing little about the place.

The city is nestled in a valley surrounded by snow-capped volcanoes sitting at up to 6,000 metres above altitude. Whilst they may be beautiful and snowy, they are also very much a live and present danger. The city lives under the constant threat of the nearest volcano, 17 kilometres away, erupting and wiping the place out. Then there is the risk of earthquakes. A real danger for it has happened many times.

Adapted as we now were to altitude, we wandered the streets of the *White City*, named after the white volcanic stone from which many of its buildings are built. The name could also apply to the reflections of the dazzling blue sky, the purest we had seen anywhere. Locals told us there is a hole in the ozone layer directly above the city, hence they have a high incidence of skin cancer, and even people with dark skins wear sunscreen.

Arequipa is a proper city, not a tourist centre like Cuzco and appeared vibrant and prosperous. It would have been interesting to have more time to get under its skin. We made do with the streets around the impressive Plaza de Armas, flanked by striking colonnades and an imposing cathedral.

In the surrounding mountains, a remarkable discovery was made a few years ago. Archaeologists found the mummified body of a young teenage girl who had been marched 500 kilometres across the Andes from Cuzco by the Incas. This cruel three months-long journey culminated in her being made a human sacrifice to the Mountain Gods.

Over 20 of these child sacrifices have been discovered to date, although Juanita the Ice Princess is the best-preserved. Even her hair remains. She has her own fascinating museum in the town centre. Whilst this might sound like a rather grizzly, almost voyeuristic, experience, it was intriguing and informative. A valuable part of understanding and interpreting the Inca story, such an integral part of life in Peru right up to this day.

The other must-do activity in Arequipa is Santa Catalina convent. When we first heard about it, we weren't sure whether to bother. *How interesting could a convent be?*

Our guidebook promised a *"Photographer's paradise,"* so we decided to give it a go. Apart from our budding young photographer Rory, who opted to stay at our hotel and watch the French Open Tennis on TV. He missed a treat.

El Monasterio de Santa Catalina was established in 1580 as a place where wealthy Spanish colonialists could send their second eldest daughter to become a nun. However, these weren't ordinary nuns. Each had a slave and their own chambers, splendid by the standards of ordinary folk. Their lifestyle was flamboyant, with slaves required to perform sexual favours for the nuns. Three hundred years later, the Vatican, always quick to cotton on, sent a strict disciplinarian to free the slaves and impose a more monastic way of life. The nuns must have had a good life, in the 17th century they had a life expectancy over 80.

A small group of nuns still live behind the walls in a section of the citadel. The remainder of the site was available for tourists to visit and take many thousands of photos every day. Wandering around this ancient complex was like being teleported to Andalucía. Bright blue and orange stone walls, wrought iron lamps, open fireplaces and citrus trees transported our senses to a small hillside town or even Seville itself. These Spanish nuns certainly did all they could to avoid homesickness.

Have you ever heard of the Colca Canyon? Me neither, to be honest, which is ridiculous. The deepest canyon in the world, at over 3,000 metres, it is twice as deep as the Grand Canyon and as high as three Scottish mountains stacked on top of one another.

The most impressive thing about this geological marvel, carved by the Rio Colca which cuts through its hundred kilometres, is not its dimensions. It is the opportunity to view, close at hand and head, the world's heaviest flying bird, the condor, with a wingspan of three metres.

Condors, revered by the Incas as a symbol of the heavens, put on a fantastic display for visitors every morning as the thermal currents rise from the canyon floor. An overnight trip from

Arequipa and a couple of early starts were needed, but what an awe-inspiring sight as these magnificent birds swooped over our heads. In front of our eyes, half a dozen majestic condor rode the currents along the valley, like Australian surfers catching a monster wave.

The only way to enjoy this experience was to join an organised tour. The drive across the Altiplano was stunning with many volcanoes, salt plains, hot springs and endless horizons. The landscape changed frequently. A few hundred metres can make a considerable difference as to what can grow and survive in a particular area.

At 4,800 metres above sea level, we were at the highest point on earth any of us had ever been. Whilst we didn't see the puma who roam these lands, we spotted plenty of llamas, alpacas, a few vicuñas, some vizcachas and a flamboyance of flamingo. For that is the collective noun for flamingo.

The people who inhabit these lands have a hard existence. The climate is harsh and the nights painfully cold. The thin air does not hold heat for long when the sun sets at this altitude. The open fire in the hotel lobby and the storage heaters in our rooms were welcome necessities as was the supply of coca tea, known locally as *mate de coca*.

In South America, we drank a great deal of *mate de coca*, brilliant for helping with the effects of altitude. Athletes can test positive for cocaine if they drink too much. We consumed plenty. It was just as well we had missed the Beijing Olympics, for I would have been disqualified.

We were getting the hang of this long-distance bus travel and made one last stop at the oasis resort of Huacachina, 12 hours overnight from Arequipa and a five hour drive to Lima Airport.

The buses had been incident free, other than my hygiene disaster on the way back from Puno. We had been warned they could be eventful. One family reported that as the lights on their bus went off for sleep time, the TV screens fired up adult movies. Thankfully, our kids' innocent eyes avoided such a spectacle.

In Western Australia, we nearly went sand-boarding. We had it all planned, but the night-time temperatures were so low we had to beat a hasty retreat from The Pinnacles to buy sleeping bags. In New Zealand, we were going to head up to Ninety Mile Beach, a sand-boarding mecca, at the top of the North Island but ran out of time. The kids were over the moon when we realised we could factor in a stopover at THE place in Peru to go sand-boarding, Huacachina.

We hadn't appreciated that most of Peru's coastal hinterland is sand. The capital city, Lima, was built on desert by the conquering Spanish colonialists who needed a port for their imperial exploits. The coastline was bleak and desolate. I can't deny that when we disembarked at Ica bus station in the cold morning fog, known as *haar* in Scotland, we seriously considered getting the next bus out of there. The fog was so thick we could hardly see the front of the bus once we had walked past it.

But our *Tripper Spirit* was strong, so we persevered, got a taxi down the road to Huacachina and checked into our hotel.

By mid-morning, the haar started to slowly clear. One by one, we began to see enormous sand dunes emerge around the palm-fringed oasis. I mean gigantic, up to 200 metres high. Imagine the Sahara Desert, with an Olympic-size swimming pool in the middle. I half expected Lawrence of Arabia to walk into the hotel lobby wearing speedos.

We had a ball, climbing up the sandy mountains and then running down barefoot, shouting and squealing with joy. Rory was in his element. This football-mad boy had not been able to run in South America. We were back at sea level. We all experienced our ears popping on the bus, but it was worth the pain to be able to run again.

Later that afternoon, Roonagh and I boarded a red and yellow beach buggy and sped out into the dunes. The ride quickly turned into a rollercoaster, the buggy not quite doing loop the loops but not far off. It drove slowly to the top of the dunes and then bombed down almost sheer vertical drops, with us screaming our heads off. I sat behind the driver so I could see what he could. Although he seemed in control, it was wild.

Sand-boarding was also a fantastic rush. You lie on your stomach on a board and down the dune you go. At speed. Fantastic fun, four times were not enough. Roonagh did have a go at standing up on the board as well, although only on gentle slopes. We didn't want another injured ankle at this late stage in our travels.

We were provided with goggles which protected our eyes from the disturbed sand flying through the air. They did their job admirably. We could have done with face masks as well. I could still feel tiny grains of sand in my teeth whilst sipping on a Pisco Sour at the *Oasis Bar* later that evening.

As Roonagh and I posed for sunset photos, proudly perched on top of the mighty dunes, I looked down at the oasis below and thought, *Yes, we did it. We absolutely nailed this. What a day, what a year, what a life.*

Roonagh looked up at me, and innocently asked, "Daddy, what's for tea?" The answer, of course, was pizza.

And that was Peru. Much like sand in an egg timer, time was running out on our year away as we savoured every remaining day. We absolutely maxed our month in Peru and left with many fond memories. Paddington Bear would have been very proud of us.

The next day we headed to Lima. A three-hour evening flight took us back to Santiago de Chile where we had started the South American leg of our travels. On this occasion, we would not venture into the city or suffer from jetlag. After a night fighting to keep awake in the departure lounge, we boarded an early morning flight across the continent to Rio de Janeiro in Brazil.

Brazil
Last orders

Two years after that casual conversation in that Turkish bar, our final destination beckoned. That city by the sea with an iconic mountain. Fifty weeks on from Cape Town, where our amazing journey began. Twenty countries. Over 100 abodes. Fifty different forms of transport. Forty carbon-emitting flights. Rio de Janeiro was the final stop on our year around the globe.

From Cape Town to Rio. We'd made it. All in one piece. Amazed at what we had experienced and where we had been. But we were absolutely cream-crackered having travelled through Peru at quite a pace. We couldn't wait to get back to Scotland. It felt like treading water. Five nights in Rio was the trip's final gift, but two nights would have been enough. We were ready for home.

We stayed on the main drag in Ipanema, five minutes from the beach and ten minutes stroll from Copacabana. An ideal location for a Rio city break. Unfortunately, the weather wasn't great, and it was the off-season in Rio. If we were to go again, it would be for the famous Carnival in February. There were a few bronzed and tanned bodies on the beach and plenty of joggers. But much like in Australia, the body shape of the average person was not what you would see on TV. Baywatch it wasn't.

The biggest shock was the language. Having had ten weeks absorbing Spanish elsewhere on the South American continent, the Brazilian Portuguese we now heard was pretty much unintelligible to our ears. It could have been Japanese for all we knew. Just like in Japan, we didn't even have a guidebook. Rio was, however, mostly self-explanatory.

A visit to the Maracanã stadium, the legendary home of Brazilian football, was non-negotiable. We found it somewhat ramshackle and needing extensive renovation ahead of the World Cup five years later. But it's not every day you get to walk in the footsteps of Pele, Kaka and John Barnes, hand in hand with your son.

The sights of Rio are terrific. The beaches yes, the mountains of course, but no doubt about it, the highlight is Christ the Redeemer. Not so much for the statue itself, as gigantic and iconic as it is. But for the view. We saved this for our final morning, 50 weeks on from when we looked down on Cape Town from Table Mountain. We finished our year by looking down on Rio and back across the Southern Atlantic Ocean to the tip of Africa where we had started. It was almost as if I had planned it that way.

I always thought we would conclude the trip with a helicopter flight over Christ the Redeemer. That flipping budget got the better of us, our funds dwindling as we made the most of the final few weeks. And neither of us had jobs to return to in recession-hit Britain. We started to convert activities into the currency of Asda shops. A helicopter ride for four would have been 11 weeks' food shopping. We could not justify that. No matter though, we were not short of once in a lifetime thrills.

And that was that. Done and dusted. Our 113th accommodation was our last. Our 39th and 40th flights awaited to take us back to the future.

With stuffed crust pizza in our stomachs, we walked hand in hand as a family along Copacabana Beach. The sun set on the final evening of the first part of our life together as a family. We had the best of times. Just as I predicted in that Turkish bar, it would impact us all, as a family and individuals, in ways we could not yet envisage.

The adventure
which kept on giving

After an incredible trip, it can sometimes feel like it never happened. There are memories, flashbacks, photos, but also a sense of illusion.

We were back home, unpacking boxes from the loft like it was Christmas Day. Surely these items belonged to someone else. We certainly didn't need them. Two rucksacks worth of belongings was all we required. We had just proved that for a whole year.

We collected the parcels of goodies we had sent to my parents whilst we were away. We unwrapped African animal guidebooks, Baobab candle holders, Boomerangs, Chinese chopsticks, Japanese wall hangings, Thai trinkets and all sorts of curiosities from the road. We had new decorations for the Christmas tree, kangaroos with Santa hats, kiwi birds and ring-tailed lemurs. These were supplemented by rugs from Ecuador, a colourful Bolivian hammock and a Brazilian bread basket, all carried in our extra tent bag on the final stages of our trip.

Roonagh had bracelets from Bali to give to her friends, and Rory wore football tops from teams around the world, none of which his friends could even recognise.

Neighbours asked, "How was your holiday?" They didn't understand. How could they? They just wanted to talk about everyday life, banal and boring things we weren't interested in. We couldn't find the words to explain what we had experienced. We didn't know where to start.

The kids disappeared into friends' houses for the summer as they just got on with it. It seemed easier for them than us over-complicated adults.

We started to edit 15,000 photos. These far-off places and exotic creatures were barely recognisable. Had we really been there? Was it just a dream? A figment of our imagination? This alchemy of memories, a mirage of reality had surely happened to somebody else. We were just an ordinary family. It felt like an out of body experience.

Over the following months, the best of these photos would start to fill our home, on desk calendars, canvas artworks, mugs and placemats. Anything that would help to remind us that we really had been around the world.

Anne had an interview during our first week back. Fortunately, she got it, a job she would keep, grow in and love for the next decade. Until she had to leave it to become a carer again, this time for Roonagh.

It was just as well Anne was working because she was the sole breadwinner. We topped up her salary with family tax credits and the occasional piece of consultancy work I managed to pick up. Returning to a severe recession, all those job opportunities

I had anticipated when we left had vanished quicker than a magician's assistant.

On his return to school after the trip, Rory's class did a project on World War II. The children were put into groups to pick a presentation topic. Rory chose to form a group of one because he wanted to do a presentation about Hiroshima. We had been there on our trip and it was poignant for him. Roonagh did a photo slide presentation to her classmates. Inevitably, most of the pictures were of cute animals. Her friends were more than a little bit envious.

We saw no adverse impact on their educational attainment when they returned to school. They were more mature and confident, which stood them in good stead as they progressed through their education.

Initially, it was difficult for them to assimilate back into school. Very quickly after our return, they stopped talking about the trip. It was almost an embarrassment for them. They needed to fit in and feel normal again. Because none of their peers could get their heads around what they had experienced, they soon put it to the back of their minds. I would annoy them periodically throughout their adolescence with comments such as "I have just had a flashback" or questions like "Who knows what we were doing on this day x years ago?"

We started to meet other travelling families from Europe and North America as they progressed on their own journeys, enjoying Scotland's beauty. They stayed with us and we exchanged stories of the road. We became lifelong friends with some, leading to future holidays in their homes. Others passed through, but each episode was a re-connection with our tripper identity.

As my year of unemployment progressed, there were times when I doubted my career would ever resume. Most days I thought, *well, if that's the cost of the trip so be it, I wouldn't swap it for anything.* There were darker moments when I wondered why we had been so reckless, but these were rare. They became more frequent when I finally got a job a year later. I was to spend four years in a role I did not enjoy. But it was all part of the process leading to me starting my own business and discovering the entrepreneur within. The risk-taker who had learnt to embrace the philosophy of "*what's the worst that can happen?*"

Starting my own business, five years after our return, was the third best decision of my life. After that bottle of Fitou and that night in a Turkish bar.

Business owners were often interested in my travel story. It connected with their own spirit of adventure, even though they could never imagine taking such a trip themselves. They would never be able to leave their business for that long. I was attracted to the idea that a business should be built to work without the owner. This goal became my focus, and seven years later, I have the flexibility to work on things I enjoy, write books and travel when we can. Overseas trips may be limited for a while because of our caring responsibilities, but this will pass, and we will head back out into the world.

The compulsive urge to travel is a recognised physical condition with its own word, dromomania. Our family caught it. It is incurable.

We have not been without unforgettable holidays in the past decade. We rarely go to just one place, instead we construct mini trips, packing in as many experiences as possible within a one or two week break. We have also taken longer breaks to

Vietnam, yes we got there eventually, the Balkans, the Baltic States, California and Cuba. The Covid-19 pandemic changed the world of work, and it became easier to run my business from anywhere. I delivered training and had sales calls from the Canary Islands. Our apartment was two minutes from a lava field. It was like being back in the Galápagos Islands. It turned out that German tourist was spot on after all, minus iguanas and giant tortoises.

The kids benefitted so much from the trip. It impacted their values and influenced their subject choices at school. When they reached the second half of their teenage years, they started to head off to far-flung places themselves. We had trained them to become backpackers, and they were ready to see the world on their own terms. Over the next few years, between them, they went to Cambodia, Central America, India, South Africa, Thailand, The Philippines, Vietnam and Mexico. Rory fell in love in Mexico and ended up moving out there to get married. Unfortunately, Roonagh fell ill with M.E. and is in the process of embarking on a long road to recovery.

I told Anne, on that fateful night in that Turkish bar, that the trip would be an investment. It turned out I was right.

"This investment will have a long-term impact on all of us, collectively and individually. I don't know what that means yet and we will find out maybe in ten years' time, but we will find out."

It took the best part of a decade, but we are there now. Our year backpacking around the world as a family fundamentally changed our outlook on life. All of us.

BONUS CHAPTER

What did you learn?

I have delivered several presentations to business networking groups about the trip, the lessons I learnt and how I applied them to growing my business. Here are a few:

- *You are capable of more than you realise*

  This ordinary family went backpacking around the world with two children. I quit my job, and the kids skipped school for a year. I still can't believe we did that. We must have been mad!

  My unexpected ability to adapt myself, chameleon-like, to the world of private enterprise after a quarter of a century as a public servant.

- *Stick to your values and purpose when the going gets tough*

  We knew why we were doing the trip. To connect us as a family and share experiences that would grow us as individuals. Our week bodyboarding in the Queensland surf was a useful reminder of getting back to basics. Back to the reason we were doing the trip in the first place.

My business has a clear purpose, to make a difference to people's lives, which helps us focus on making the right choices and decisions. Building a business is not a straight line, there are many twists and turns along the way, but if you stay true to yourself, your purpose and values, you should be ok.

- *What's the worst that can happen?*

    I did bring my father's grandchildren home safely, I did get a job in the end, and we didn't need to downsize the house.

    I did build the business, I didn't have to get another job, and I am happy.

- *You choose the journey and the destination*

    Bookends, Cape Town to Rio. One year, fast-moving, but with plenty of down days for family time.

    Lifestyle or growth business? Just me, or a team that would have fulfilling jobs and work on my behalf? Either way, make sure you enjoy it. If you don't, do something else.

- *You can picture the future, but it will be different when you get there*

    Machu Picchu was different for a sickly me than I had imagined, just as it was for our American friends with their stroppy teenager.

I thought I would know what my business would look like at this stage, but I could never imagine how it would feel, the complex bundle of emotions like imposter syndrome, my inner critic and self-sabotage.

- *The importance of team identity and bond*

  The Family Trippers, us against the world. That name and the identity that came with it helped keep us right at times and forged *Tripper Spirit*.

  My team are so close and tight-knit. They have each other's backs and won a Scottish Employer of the Year award in 2020. I am proud of them.

- *Know your numbers*

  That eventful train journey to Kyoto provided ample evidence that understanding your financial position matters. By facing up to the reality of my mistake, we were able to adjust our outgoings and along with a healthy dose of luck, still make things work.

  As someone who only passed his Maths exam at school, because his mother made it clear that he would keep re-taking it until he did, business finance has been a massive learning curve. But I have also known from day one the criticality of being on top of my numbers and metrics.

- *You never know what you will write*

  I often had writer's block with the blogs, but by and large, the words flowed once I got around to sitting down with my laptop. Generally speaking, they were pretty decent. I am so glad I wrote them, they have been a terrific source of inspiration and provided a contemporaneous record for me to draw on in writing this book.

It has been the same with reports, training courses and sales proposals, I don't know where they come from sometimes, but generally, they are pretty good.

- *Same Same but Different*

   This Thai truism played out as we moved from continent to continent, seeing different versions of the same thing, maybe with a subtle twist here and there.

   When you start a business, everything is new, but you build experience that will stand you in good stead over time and begin to see similar things and trends. Just as our travel savvy skills improved day by day, so did my business acumen year by year.

- *Opportunity springs from adversity*

   Every time something went wrong on the trip, something good happened as a result. Look at the impact of the China earthquake, for example. Apart from the Giant Panda Odyssey which didn't end well.

   It has been the same with the business, every time we lose a client, we end up getting a bigger and better one.

- *Most people are good people*

  Scams were much rarer than kindness and generosity. For every Ecuadorian paint pourer, there were hundreds of Hill Tribe villagers. For every Chinese taxi driver, there was a Madagascan conservationist who would give up his afternoon to take excited kids back to feed ring-tailed lemurs at sunset.

  For every rotten apple in a business, the employee who is "*at it*," there will be hundreds of good people who just want to come to work to do a good job, have some fun, develop themselves, have social contact and get paid.

- *Research Research Research*

  It's all very well being spontaneous, but a little bit of knowledge always goes a long way. Japan was amazing, but it would have been better with a guidebook. If we had known that Santiago doesn't do Easter, would we have gone?

  Never turn up to sales meetings unprepared. You don't know how it will go until you get there, but your chances of bagging the deal are bound to be better if you have done your prep.

- *Planning is good, but so is reacting*

  We often found a better option when we talked to people on the ground, rather than the plan we had researched. Plan A, B and even C are rarely the best one. Plan D rocks! Whether that is going to the Galápagos Islands after all or getting Rafa

Nadal's autograph when we were only in Melbourne for its airport.

You might start with an HR business, and then find that you also provide Health and Safety services as well, just because the opportunity presented itself and you grabbed it with both hands.

- *Have a backup plan*

    Back up your photos of Bangkok before you delete them. That way you won't have to do a madcap tour to recapture them. And always regret that you will never get back those jaw-dropping images of Angkor Wat.

    Have an annual business plan, but then keep it flexible. The only thing you can confidently expect is that the unexpected will happen. You might have a business plan prepared for 2020 and then find that a pandemic hits, so you have to be agile.

- *Keep on Keeping on*

    Even when your knee is throbbing with pain on the Great Wall of China. Or you're fighting a tropical disease and don't think you will be able to see the sun rise over Machu Picchu. That's what *Tripper Spirit* is all about.

    Or when you fear that your business will never make money and wonder why you were so stupid as to give up a secure job with a final salary pension. Keep going, you are making progress, you just can't see the impact of your hard work yet.

- *You take yourself with you*

  You can be in the most exotic places on Earth and still experience the same insecurities or doubts you would have back home. You can be putting up a tent alongside a stunning riverside location and still have a barnstorming argument with the woman you love. You can have more money in your bank account than your taxi driver makes in a decade and still argue over a dollar.

  When you run a business or lead a team, you have a choice. Shall I be true to myself, be who I am and be authentic? Or shall I try and play the role I think is expected of me? Do the former, be yourself. As the saying goes, everyone else is taken.

- *And Have Fun!*

  You're a long time dead. You might only go around this planet 80 times or less, so make them the best years you can. Do your work, make a difference to people, don't adversely impact the planet whenever possible and enjoy yourself.

  On my journey on earth, from a baby in a nappy to an old man, sitting in a rocking chair, in a nappy, I hope I will achieve all of this.

  I will have a magical set of memories to look back on, for as long as I can remember them.

  I wish that for my now grown-up children as well. And their children's children too. I hope they will read this book and take notes.

About the Author

Ian Pilbeam is addicted to travel. When he is not running his Human Resources and Health & Safety business in his adopted hometown of Edinburgh, he is always planning the next trip. The biggest trip of all was the year his family went around the world in 2008/09. That let the genie out of the bottle, and it will never go back in.

Having grown up in Boston, Lincolnshire, he met his Scottish wife-to-be on the Isle of Wight. Via a circuitous route, they moved up to Scotland at the start of the Millennium, with a toddler and a bump, and have never left. Apart from when they are away.

Contact details

Please get in touch via familytrippers.co.uk.

To see places and people in this book, you can find us on Instagram.com/originalfamilytrippers

Printed in Great Britain
by Amazon

58100926R00158